GO
BEYOND

NEVILLE PRITCHARD
AND RICHARD SCOTT

authorHOUSE®

AuthorHouse™ UK
1663 Liberty Drive
Bloomington, IN 47403 USA
www.authorhouse.co.uk
Phone: 0800.197.4150

Published by AuthorHouse 03/21/2018

ISBN: 978-1-5462-9014-8 (sc)
ISBN: 978-1-5462-9015-5 (hc)
ISBN: 978-1-5462-9013-1 (e)

Go Beyond—Determine Your Path towards Impact People Support
Your Workplace = Your World

CONTENTS

FOREWORD

This is the moment.

If you are a fellow people person, then this is your moment for *going beyond.*

By the words "people person", I mean any professional concerned with human performance—and human potential—in organisations. Examples include professionals engaged in HR, Learning, Organisation Development, Talent Development, and more.

Pritchard and Scott note that the people profession is in revolution. Executives, scholars, professional societies, and others are pointing to the poor performance of our profession and questioning the very need for it—at least in its current form. The most common criticisms include its lack of business relevance and its inability to provide solutions to urgent business problems. Pritchard and Scott also note that the emerging business environment is offering our profession an unprecedented opportunity to provide real value—if it, and we, will go beyond.

The global economy and the unrelenting competition it enables has created a working environment that can be incredibly hard on people. This fast-moving, constantly changing, and unpredictable environment has become so complex that scholars are creating new terms to describe various pieces of it. Examples include "permanent white water",[1] "wicked problems",[2] "adaptive challenges",[3] and my personal favourite, "VUCA"—an acronym for volatile, uncertain, complex, and ambiguous.[4]

A key characteristic of the new environment is an increase in the volume and complexity of problems. In addition, we are seeing the emergence of a new type of problem that is both more complex and different from anything encountered before. These "wicked" problems are so different that nothing in our experience is relevant to their solution—and, in fact, they may have no solution. Small wonder that people in organisations can become overwhelmed and disengaged.

A few years ago, I was attending a professional conference at which the results of Gallup's 2013 Global Workforce Study were being discussed. The speaker noted that only 13 per cent of people in 143 countries reported that they were engaged in their work—while some 24 per cent reported they were actively disengaged. From the back of the room, someone said in a loud voice, "Imagine the impact of this on global productivity." In response, I heard myself say, "Imagine the impact on the quality of work life of millions." Millions. This brings me back to our profession and to the opportunity now facing it. Can we help people and organisations navigate in the new environment? Can we create and implement new programs that go beyond best-in-class thinking to help people and organisations achieve their potential? Can we go beyond analytics to insight?

---

[1] P. B. Vaill, *Learning as a Way of Being: Strategies for Survival in a World of Permanent Whitewater* (San Francisco: Jossey-Bass, 1996).

[2] K. Grint, "Wicked Problems and Clumsy Solutions: The Role of Leadership", *Clinical Leader*, 1/2, 11–25.

[3] R. A. Heifetz, A. Grashow, and M. Linsky, "Leadership in a Permanent Crisis", *Harvard Business Review*, 87 (July–Aug. 2009), 62–69.

[4] B. Johansen, *Get There Early: Sensing the Future to Compete in the Present* (San Francisco: Berrett-Koehler, 2007).

In the pages that follow, Pritchard and Scott discuss the new environment, our profession, and offer suggestions for taking our profession to the next level. They note that old solutions and best practices are not enough. New thinking, fresh insight, and fast experimentation will be needed. They also assert that taking our profession to the next level will require more from us individually: our full energy, our best thinking, our highest performance, and our commitment. It will require going beyond.

—Walter McFarland

Co-author of *Choosing Change*; Board Chair Emeritus, ATD; and Global Lead, Human and Organisational Potential, North Highland

ACKNOWLEDGEMENTS

Go Beyond has taken a while to complete, largely because of the moving landscape of organisational development and, Human Resources, and the people agenda in recent times. Throughout we have been indebted to the support from our research assistant Chloe Amies. As well as the research support, we have appreciated the encouragement, drafting, editing, and nudging she has given us. *Go Beyond* would still be in concept stage without her support. Throughout, she has, in turn, been encouraged and supported by People in Flow Operations Director Zoë Gardner. While in that role, Zoë also created the time to enable Neville to write. Canada will be lucky to have her working there now.

We are also grateful for the time, expertise, and support gained in the early stages from Peter Casebow and his team at Good Practice for their contributions in research and the "Valued to Valuable" paper developed by Neville and Peter in 2015 which formed the foundation for this book.

We would also like to thank those interviewed and all who completed questionnaires and surveys to inform us of current thinking and activity. There are too many to mention individually, but your contributions were welcome and much appreciated.

We also thank the team at HR in Flow Ltd and People in Flow Ltd, especially Jon, Simon, Calypso, Rae, Kelsey and Nigel for your support through the research, note making periods and read-throughs.

Finally, a thank-you to our networks at the Chartered Institute of Personnel and Development, the Learning and Performance Institute, the Society for Human Resource Management and the Association for Talent Development, through which we met many who have helped to shape and inform this project. We highly recommend that professionals in this field join their respective local organisations and get involved. You need to see what is happening now and explore the possible if you are to conquer new fields and challenges.

Go Beyond contains public sector information licensed under the Open Government Licence v3.0.

INTRODUCTION

There is a lot of speculation, research, views, and theory surrounding the future of Human Resources (HR). Considerations include whether it should be called something else, defining what is and what is not part of it, and what it might look like, and focus upon, in the future. Our research seeks to go beyond the view from those inside the world of HR. At this point, though, here are some simple questions on the current state of HR:

Why does HR—in whatever form and shape—exist now?
- Is it to defend or to contribute?
- Is it for the company or the individual staff member?
- Is it to tick boxes and comply, or to make a difference?
- Is it to deliver or to provide?
- Is it to manage or to enable?
- Is it training/recruitment or performance that needs to be measured?
- Should it take orders or provide consultative influence?
- Are managers and leaders beyond reach, or do they need support and advice?
- Is HR to be respected or to be ignored; to be tolerated or governed?

Are these dilemmas or questions enhanced by adding the word "and" in place of or alongside "or"?

Where do we need to go beyond, and how? We need to go beyond the job description and role profile in recruitment to ensure "fit". We need to go beyond the catalogue of training to enable people to access learning as they need it in the form that helps most. We need to go beyond the monitoring of performance to the taking of responsibility for our part in an informed, integrated, collaborative, and coordinated approach to performance, going beyond the standard appraisal to find what works for us. We need to go beyond standard analytics. We need to go beyond management to involve all. We need to go beyond the standard processes and systems to make things work efficiently *and* effectively. We need to go beyond compliance and make an impact. We need to go beyond engagement to get a "benchmark award" and get into the detail on detachment, resilience, and motivation. We need to go beyond change to the transformation and then the continuous reinforcement of the working environment that best achieves for us. We need to go beyond physical well-being to include mental health.

The discussion that follows each of the questions above helps to define the existing organisation culture and its wrap-around values. Our research has provided deep insights into the various subcultures that exist in organisations and how they need to be framed within engagement, detachment, change readiness, experience, management, and departmental assessments.

Both authors are committed to ensuring that HR attains the status it deserves, or rather should earn, as a highly valuable resource within any organisation. As a result, we are concerned that HR professionals often do their specialisation an injustice by obscuring their message with jargon and specialised language which means nothing to a non-HR audience. Promising initiatives are smothered by terminology which merely confirms the belief of non-HR colleagues in their belief that HR specialists inhabit a parallel universe which has little or no connection with the real world.

All of us in HR must stop undermining ourselves by cloaking good ideas in our own jargon, stop playing into the hands of those who treat such "HR-speak" as a joke, and start speaking the same language as everyone else. The authors are therefore making every effort, in this book and elsewhere, to persuade HR colleagues to adopt language tailored to their audience to show that they are as grounded as anyone else in the work of their organisations, and to enable HR to acquire the status it deserves as a valuable business partner.

We also address the growing importance of HR analytics, the analysis and interpretation of people data to provide the basis for business decisions. In addition to enabling better-informed decision-making, this further contributes to the effort to elevate HR from its perceived fluffy and otherworldly nature, a view held by some colleagues outside HR, to a status equal with any other essential element of an organisation. In doing so, we will go beyond standard data and explore the sources of information that can make a significant difference.

What's in a name?

Organisations engaged in making employees redundant often describe themselves as "shedding jobs". Not getting rid of *people*, you notice, but dispensing with *posts*, as if this were a purely paper exercise, and not something which will affect the lives of real people. Dehumanising people in this way is simply a pretty clumsy way of trying to obscure the reality of an unpleasant situation, and is exactly the opposite of the clarity we are seeking.

The title Human Resources came about in an attempt to show that an organisation's people are essential business resources in the same way as its vehicles or IT. Unfortunately, a move which was aimed at showing people as special has backfired to some extent, in that the "resources" element of the title has become more prominent than the "human" part.

Some people claim that the title doesn't matter, that the words aren't important. We disagree. Strongly, as it happens. If you have ever heard, as we certainly have, the sarcastic tone used by some people to pronounce the title "HR", or seen them use their hands to mark out irritating imaginary quotation marks around the words "human resources", then you would feel, as we do, that the language really does matter. No one seems to sneer or roll their eyes when referring to Sales or Marketing, because their titles simply describe what those departments do. Our specialisation, on the other hand, has saddled itself with a title which plays into the hands of those who write the function off as full of jargon and little else. Anything which allows people to make a joke out of the very name of our specialisation can only serve to undermine us professionally.

Let's not lose sight of the fact that a function title is primarily for external use, as it were. Those who work in a function know perfectly well what it does, but the title needs to be clear to those outside that area of an organisation. Those of us who have never worked in production, sales, or marketing nevertheless have a pretty shrewd idea of what goes on in those departments, because the words on the door give us a good clue. Does the title "human resources" do the same?

Let's stop provoking sarcasm and chuckles at our own expense and come up with a function title which simply says what we do. Whoever starts this debate is sure to attract criticism in bucketloads, but let's grasp the nettle and go beyond slavish current practice for a moment and suggest the term "People Support". You need to be what you are for your company. For example, alternatives could include "people impact and contribution", "people improvement and development", "people and performance", and "people support and development". Whatever the title of the department, it should reflect its intended role and contribution. For this book, we are going to include these ideas under the heading of "people support", with the intention of providing greater impact from supporting our people. We don't make stuff, sell it, or tell potential customers how good it is. We look after the people in our organisation, for the benefit of the organisation. We recruit them, train them to continue to perform or respond to new challenges as needed, ensure their safety in the workplace, safeguard their and the organisation's legal rights, and deal with all the problems which can crop up along the way. We *support* them, in fact, so why not tell the world exactly that? Why not have a title which is a straightforward description of what we do? We also have a sneaking suspicion that most employees, whatever organisation they work for, would prefer to be described as people, rather than a resource.

The linking of organisation development and employee relations activity, and the complexity involved in aligning them for the benefit of *all* involved in achieving organisation results, is critical in defining current structures and priorities. Because of this, it is also relevant in the exploration of the future of work and future needs from HR—essentially, people support.

One component currently under-managed by the people professionals within organisations is that of management impact on all people measures. In discussion with one employee relations outsource company, it emerged that they take over **3,000** support calls per day, **70** per cent of which are related to grievances and discipline. The simple cost of the time involved in such volumes of "negative impact" activity flags a need for greater powers of action within people support to address the causal factors. This includes the need for seriously considered individual and departmental 360 reviews, the deeper analysis of results, and the committed management of the issues identified. The manager or executive badge does not exonerate anyone from responsibility for people performance. We will explore the manager balance sheet, something HR and people support functions need to drive to ensure responsibility is taken.

HR must go beyond itself now to meet future challenges, and not simply by being agile or commercial or inclusive; it is the internal ability to go beyond with impact people support, including the use of genuinely insightful support, that will make a difference.

The expertise in people support, development, and optimisation is not constrained now, and will not be constrained in the future, by a departmental name or the focus of internal staff within that function. It is the taking of responsibility for the culture within, for enabling consistent and situational application of values by and with management, and for the provision of expertise rather than simple service, that will map the future of work and HR.

CHAPTER 1

PEOPLE SUPPORT CENTRE

Beyond fundamentals and strategy

Why do people-support departments, teams, or functions exist? Why human resources, organisation development, learning/ training, talent, leadership development, recruitment, reward, etc.?

We will explore these throughout the book, but we need a starting point. Strategy derived from organisation direction is our starting point. Yet we need to go beyond strategy and, as Alex Evans notes in his book *The Myth Gap*, consider what happens when evidence and arguments are not enough. The strategy developed by people support (i.e., all people-related functions) must derive from and support the achievement of the overall organisation strategy, purpose, and intent. For that to happen, people-related functions need to own the defining, shaping, management, and enabling of workplace people activity, the environment, culture, norms, and checks against purpose. People in Flow Ltd is a company that encourages organisations to do what is right for themselves, promoting the concept YOUR WORKPLACE = YOUR WORLD (2017 - People in Flow).

To be fair, most of the functions contributing to our research are indeed attempting to do so at the highest level. Thereafter, challenges exist.

There are the tactical demands of executive and senior managers and a few noisy and opinionated middle managers. Middle managers may solutioneer (as one of the authors has referred to it) the actions and priorities with reference not to strategy but to the immediate situation. The answer-before-the-question approach often results in a defensive action. We hear a lot about HR transformation, yet upon review, we see that much of this is restricted by the current state and the demands of other business managers and their perceptions of the role of people support. If we ask the tough questions, then we should be prepared to work with the answers. Thus, for change to really happen for the benefit of all, then *all* should be included in the strategic considerations. For there to be a transformation in the way people contribute, they need to be involved. How the culture is brought to life is dependent on how well that inclusion is delivered. What do you really need? What really matters?

What then of consulting firm recommendations, especially, as mentioned, those who come with an answer and look for the question; those relying upon data to drive change; those working with senior management and their potentially self-interested insight? In setting aligned strategy, it is important when leading people support and related functions not to be swayed by fashion, fads, product placement or fitting.

All can have a say in determining what culture will drive results. All can positively or negatively impact achievement. The subtitle of this book, *Your Workplace = Your World*, identifies the extent to which people are at, travelling to and from, or simply thinking about work, as far exceeding time on other pursuits. With sleep included, your workplace matters. People support should not be handing out escape clauses to managers or employees when it comes to earning what they are paid and taking responsibility for the working environment and culture. We should not open the door for blaming others with the opportunity to judge others rather than focusing on personal performance.

We also suggest the need to recognise that every organisation is different. The small groups that influence performance and culture are different. Lazy people-support leadership cannot move things forward. The newly appointed head from another company, intent on doing what he or she did there as perceived established success without gaining deep insight, is again adopting the approach of the answer seeking the question!

Basic commercial thinking suggests you establish the questions and then reach the right answer for your organisation, cognisant of all that is current that may help. Good consulting can help maintain that objectivity. You need to be sure it is objective.

Going beyond strategy means looking first at what you have and what is happening, and then making sense of that before overlaying the organisation's intent. Then you consider who will best influence the strategy adoption at every level, when and where you can achieve positive influence, and how you drive change. Questions are the starting point.

So what questions should people support directors/heads of people support and related functions be asking themselves? Examples include the following:

Question	Response
What is the overall business plan?	
Have we established a clear set of wrap-around values within which our culture and subcultures can grow?	
Are we structurally focused on the intent and purpose?	
What is the business balance of spend?	
What are the income challenges?	
How aligned is our people strategy?	

Are we encouraging the learning needed to achieve our intent? Is there any?	
Are we recruiting as well as we can for this organisation now?	
What data do I have and do I need?	
What data will help others?	
What is or should be the raison d'être for people support, including development?	
What should be the manifesto?	
Where are we adding most connectivity and value?	
Where are the problems in terms of disconnections with other business leaders?	
Where is the real value potential?	
What are we for?	
What needs to change in the wider organisation for change within the people support and development roles to succeed in adding value?	
What wider benefits are the potential prize from change?	

When taking an initial snapshot of the people-support functions within any organisation, we initially get a feel for the current state, the mindset, the expectations, and the perceived role by plotting the functional team sheet. In other words, what is the key purpose of each sub-function? Is it defence, midfield, or attack? This gives a quick view on the current balance of activity, time allocation, resource focus, and wider organisational mindset.

So should people support focus on compliance or value add or both? Are those within people support currently perceived by management as people who are experts with contributions that could add value? It can help to view the roles within people support functions as sport teams with defensive, creative midfield, or attacking potential. Consider your people support departments, teams, and functions. Which position would they fulfil? Each has a different value. Each needs a different kind of expertise. Focusing on value may help our perception.

As an example, a European technology company recently conducted an audit on processes developed centrally. Following a 'failed audit' a need for training was identified by the compliance and HR teams. When a consultant investigated, training was far from being needed; they all knew the processes. In their specific situation and geography the processes would not work. What was needed was a review meeting at which informed and collaborative management and practitioners could explore the right way for the company. There was a need to go beyond knowledge to applied wisdom.

People are really *assets*, especially when released or enabled to add their full potential value. They should not simply be resources to be "managed". We like the approach within a leading social media and global communication company, where everyone is expected to play to their strengths every day. They are empowered to be their best. This does not mean that "entitlement" should reign and that there is no need for leadership or that activity doesn't need some form of framework. But it does mean that micromanagement is not required!

So what is required?

➢ What skills are required of those within the people support (including development) functions?
➢ What external support will add value?
➢ How do we integrate everything to create greater impact?

To provide further context, an article in *People Management* stated, "HR 'lacks skills to become more strategic' despite major changes."[1]

---

[1] Grace Lewis, "HR 'Lacks Skills to Become More Strategic' despite Major Changes," *People Management* (13 February 2013.

It goes on to say, "HR professionals are not developing the right skills to cope with changing HR operating models, a report from the CIPD has found."

This is despite restructuring in half of HR and people support departments to support a more strategic approach in the past two years. The Institute said that practitioners were failing to develop "business savvy and commercial expertise" that would enable them to become strategic contributors to their business.

Although the role of the HR business partner has become more prevalent in recent years, the latest Chartered Institute of Personnel and Development (CIPD) HR Outlook Survey[2] suggests that professionals need greater specialist skills, such as commercial acumen, data awareness, and data analysis, to really bring value to their organisation in the future. The survey asked 630 HR professionals what the current state of the profession is and how HR professionals and employers are reacting to emerging trends. From the findings, it can be gleaned that "working with the organisation to drive change" is the most important area for HR to focus on, but just 76 per cent said that HR understands how the organisation works and how people practices influence the value chain.

In the same survey, just 16 per cent of junior HR practitioners felt they needed to combine commercial and HR expertise to bring value to the organisation, compared to 27 per cent of more senior HR professionals. Dr Jill Miller, research advisor at the CIPD, said this was evidence that professionals aren't developing the necessary skills early enough in their careers, prompting employers to consider new HR operating models.

---

[2] Chartered Institute of Personnel and Development, *HR Outlook: Winter 2016–2017: Views of Our Profession*, https://www.cipd.co.uk/Images/hr-outlook_2017_tcm18-17697.pdf, with the permission of the publisher, the Chartered Institute of Personnel and Development, London (www.cipd.co.uk)

Regardless of the operating model an organisation chooses, HR has a crucial role to play in bringing unique insights about the organisation's people to business debates, informing strategic decision-making.

Action around HR analytics is an essential way in which HR professionals can develop this commercial mindset, inform the people agenda, and increase visibility of HR's impact on the business's key performance indicators. Similarly, an awareness of the evolution of the profession is vital.

Almost half of HR directors surveyed said their last job role was outside HR, and 70 per cent of HR directors had worked in roles outside HR five job roles ago. This suggests that time spent learning elsewhere in the business or rotating in and out of HR could be valuable in reaching a senior HR position, the CIPD said. Peter Cheese, chief executive of the CIPD, said "agility" had become the watchword for the profession.

"HR professionals should be constantly evaluating their job role and finding ways in which they can adapt to the evolving work environment. The CIPD profession map is a great place to start, as it can help professionals to focus on building skills that will allow their role to evolve with the industry around them and open up all potential career pathways," he said.

We believe the profession map to be an excellent starting point, yet there is a need to see this through a different lens. All that is within it is high-quality consideration, material, and effort.

In addition to more efficiently managing the compliance and housekeeping elements, we see the organisation development components within people support as the potential for the most radical transformation. Thus, the shift in thinking, who needs to adapt, when and where the potential levers of change can be delivered, and how to approach transformation, are all covered in this book.

"If you want to succeed you should strike out on new paths, rather than travel the worn paths of accepted success."

—John D. Rockefeller

We have worked with organisations varying in size from 5 employees up to 180,000. In doing so, we have seen many examples of the misuse and blind faith shown in the worn paths of accepted success, being quoted as "best practice". That which is really common practice is not always right for specific and uniquely different organisations. And are they really paths of success?

We will explore examples within appropriate chapters.

People support (HR)—the people analysis, development, and support framework

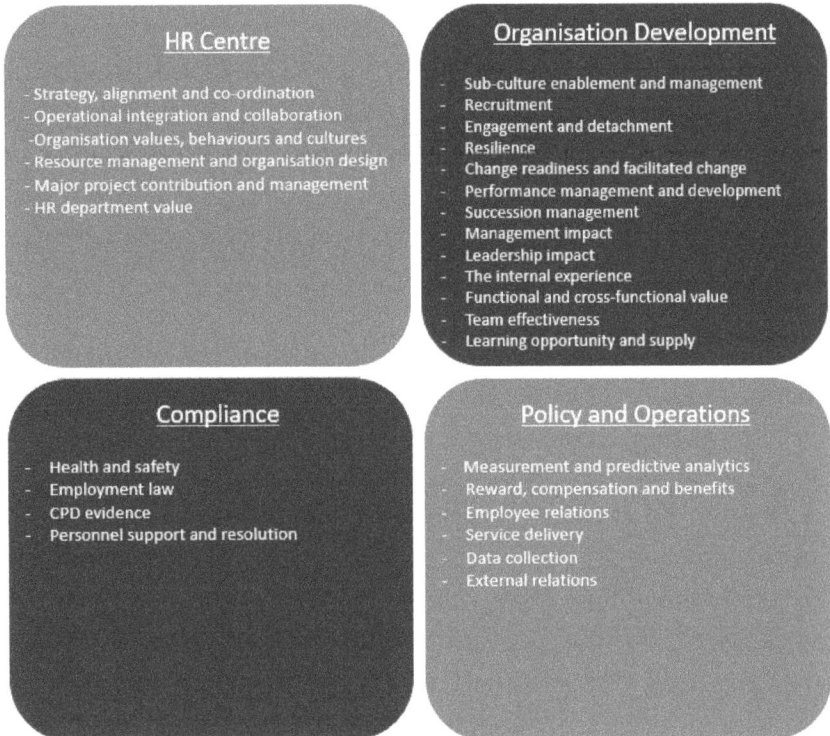

HR Centre

- Strategy, alignment and co-ordination
- Operational integration and collaboration
- Organisation values, behaviours and cultures
- Resource management and organisation design
- Major project contribution and management
- HR department value

Organisation Development

- Sub-culture enablement and management
- Recruitment
- Engagement and detachment
- Resilience
- Change readiness and facilitated change
- Performance management and development
- Succession management
- Management impact
- Leadership impact
- The internal experience
- Functional and cross-functional value
- Team effectiveness
- Learning opportunity and supply

Compliance

- Health and safety
- Employment law
- CPD evidence
- Personnel support and resolution

Policy and Operations

- Measurement and predictive analytics
- Reward, compensation and benefits
- Employee relations
- Service delivery
- Data collection
- External relations

We need to redefine newer definitions such as that of OD to unleash pragmatism in areas such as learning and development.

Our view is that the purpose of people support is to ensure an informed, integrated, collaborative, and coordinated management and to enable all people-performance expectations. This is to be achieved within the operating culture needed and the requirements of related legislation. People support needs to go beyond the commonly held perception of itself. Possibly a somewhat "tick box" perception is necessary for the "defence" role of people support in a company. Very often we need to shift this perception. To do so, we need to be clear on what is intended and needed, and then reclarify what activities—and with them, the necessary data feeds—are needed.

The possibility of ensuring an informed, integrated, collaborative, and coordinated service, with other organisation leaders fulfilling defined "people" responsibilities, is significantly improved if we implement it with a three-stage mindset:

1. Gain **insight**.
2. Generate **impact**.
3. Enable **flow**.

Examples of behavioural needs associated with such a management approach could include an energised environment and engaged people, high trust/low stress, responsibility-focused norms, and a commitment to others.

So, within this given context, the challenges facing people support strategy are many. We note those most common in the remainder of this chapter.

What is a balanced and impactful people strategy? Is it the performance shortfall establishing a "total performance" organisation?

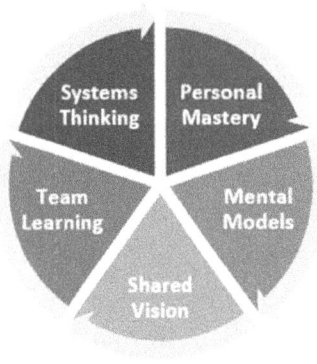

Peter Senge's Five Disciplines

Peter Senge and colleagues introduced the concept of the learning organisation in the book *The Fifth Discipline*[3] in the early 1990s.

Senge stops short of really defining the key to the successful deployment of a committed learning organisation, which is the motivation required for the learning to happen. A shared vision needs to materialise as shared and agreed intent.

Organisations need to use performance to focus on achievement and gather learning to ensure continuous sustainability and improvement.

A Total Performance Organisation is one that is result- and performance-focused; recognises the journey to the result; realises the need for coordinated performance from many sources to achieve intent; and continuously learns from performance to achieve results in the way in which it would wish to.

In our opinion, the considerations behind ensuring a strong people support build and then developing strategy can be divided into five steps, and then followed by action:

- Start with the business.
- Achieve operational excellence.
- Ensure dynamic contribution.

---

[3] Peter Senge, *The Fifth Discipline: The art and practice of the learning organization* (2nd edn, Random House Business, 2006).

- Increase organisational energy.
- Enjoy insight, impact, and flow.

Framing impact people support

Start with the business

"There continues to be a perception that commercial acumen is in short supply within the HR function, and frustration on the part of senior executives that HR is somehow falling short of the full contribution it could make to business success."[4]

Most of us have heard the story. President Kennedy was visiting the NASA Space Centre at Cape Canaveral in 1962 when he encountered a man with a broom. He asked the man what his job was, and he replied: "I'm helping to put a man on the moon." This man had an admirably clear idea of exactly what his organisation was all about, and precisely how his own role contributed to that. NASA's priority at that time was the *Apollo* programme, designed to do exactly what the man described.

Unfortunately, all too many people support professionals are rather less clear about how they fit in. They tend to believe that their role is to support the employees, full stop. They see their job as being to recruit the right people, place them in appropriate jobs, train them, look after their welfare, safeguard their health and safety, and help them to achieve a good work–life balance. These things are certainly all part and parcel of their job, but the job doesn't stop or even start there. *All* those activities, and more, form part of the varied, challenging, and rewarding work of the people support professional, but *all* of them must be directly aligned with the overall purpose of the organisation, and with a view to the way in which these people support activities affect business performance.

---

[4] Corporate Research Forum, *Developing Commercial Acumen* (2013).

"Start with the business" expresses the need to understand clearly the purpose of the organisation as a first step towards understanding how people support can contribute to that purpose. People support is there to serve the organisation's purpose, whether that is to build aircraft, make cars, sell insurance, fit tyres, or run public libraries.

"HR needs to understand the business in which they operate and be clear about the linkages between HR actions and business outcomes."[5]

No one would question the fact that the marketing department exists to serve the organisation's purpose and achieve its aims, and similarly with the sales or production departments (where these exist, depending on the nature of the organisation). The people support department is no different. Serving the organisation's purpose requires an understanding of the business and the environment in which it operates, to ensure that one's work consistently serves the bottom line. Only in this way will people support become a truly valuable part of the organisation, seen as being of genuinely strategic importance and whose contribution to performance is obvious.

"In many organisations, there are doubts about HR's business knowledge and the relevance of some of its activities."[6]

People support professionals need to follow the advice of one chief human resources officer, quoted in a Deloitte survey in 2016,[7] who tells HR leaders to "spend time where the company makes money" in order to really understand the business.

---

[5] Corporate Research Forum, *Developing Commercial Acumen* (2013).

[6] Ibid.

[7] Deloitte, *Global Human Capital Trends 2016: The new organization: Different by design* (Deloitte University Press, 2016).

Starting with the business calls for an understanding of the purpose of the organisation; the industry/sector in which it operates; the context in which it operates (local, national, and/or global); where the organisation is in its spiral of growth; who the customers are; who the employees are; how the organisation is internally aligned, integrated, managed, and organised for impact (AIMI); the extent of clarity of purpose and intent; how people support professionals communicate with the rest of the organisation; how people support contributes to the organisation's performance; how it could contribute more; and the collective feel needed to achieve as an organisation. Furthermore, it will need to appreciate the objectives, actions, and results required at all four levels (individual, team, function, organisation); understand the expected contribution of every role; recognise where time can be created to enable focus; know where the levers of performance are; and know what matters most to the people within the organisation.

If we look at each of these points in more detail, we see that "start with the business" is much more than an empty mantra.

The purpose of the organisation

Absolute clarity of purpose is needed here, together with a robust interpretation of what is and is not relevant. People support professionals must be clear about the fundamental purpose of their organisation, and robust enough to ensure that everything they do is aligned with that purpose. This does not involve adopting a ruthless style of people management which would suit a Dickensian factory owner, but it simply amounts to ensuring that everything we do serves the business.

When we explore learning and development, we will see that employees are trained to enable them to perform their jobs, and to do them better than they currently do. They may be trained to expand or adjust the focus of their work to meet new market demands. The purpose and objectives of training in any medium are too often listed and communicated from the trainer or developer perspective—a way that *they* can check whether they are achieving their goals for delivery. These are of zero consequence to the learner. Learners need to know why they are learning, what they are going to learn, what difference it will make to them, whom it will impact, when it is relevant, and how they may access the learning to improve, change, adjust, or refine their performance.

Learning links with performance and managers, leaders, and colleagues can then ensure learning is transferred to the workplace. The framework is one of a performance management approach in any organisation. It is not a system or a process. It is a continual collective action.

In this picture, everything we do needs to start from an informed base, and then be integrated, coordinated, and developed collaboratively to ensure maximum impact. Thus, performance management incorporates leadership and management style, and clarity of purpose and intent for all roles, teams, and functions, as part of the overall purpose. It also encompasses opportunity for development, reward that reinforces and encourages performance, formal and informal cultural support, and an energy for enabling success. This is, then, more than a tick box, smart objectives, or an online rating system. If confined to a people support system to deliver the tool, then this is what it tends to be. If started with the business, and if it totally embraces the organisation's purpose and all are tuned towards achievement, then it will be a more valuable and positively applied habit, one that can transform performance. We will explore this further when looking at performance in more detail.

The industry/sector in which the organisation operates
Is it a specialised, niche market, or a more general sector? Who are the competitors (if any)? Which are the greatest threats? Who is

making what innovation? Where will the industry be in five years, or even one year in this fast-moving world? How does people support match the pace of the organisation and the industry? Taking Facebook, Google, and other tech companies as examples—they do what is needed when it is needed, and create, sustain, and protect their culture.

The context in which the organisation operates (local, national, and/ or global)

Does the organisation cover a specific geographical area (like a local authority, for example), or serve customers anywhere? What proportion of its business is conducted online? How is technology affecting the business? What new developments are imminent? What is likely to impact the access to talent? Where are the people the organisation will need next year?

Where the organisation is in its spiral of growth

Where is it in terms of the wealth-dynamic cycle? What phase of the business cycle is it in and about to enter, and what energies need to dominate? Where are the new markets? Are there plans for expansion? Or contraction/reorganisation? How will this affect people support? How can people support contribute?

Who the customers are

The marketing department will profile the organisation's customers. Gaining an insight into this work will help you to understand the business, and at the same time show colleagues in another department that you are eager to understand the wider context of your work. What impact on customer experience can the operating frameworks supported by people support have for customers? How can people support improve this impact?

Who the employees are

Many organisations spend huge sums profiling their customers in detail, but they pay much less attention to finding out about their own people. Professor Paul Sparrow[8] describes a strategic planning meeting at Tesco at which the CEO heard a detailed analysis of the firm's customers given by the marketing department, followed by a very pedestrian set of unremarkable statistics about the staff, and then commented: "We seem to know more about our customers than we do our workforce." Tesco is very unlikely to be the only organisation to have found itself in this situation. Understanding the employees is the key to ensuring that they are trained, organised, and deployed in the best interests of the organisation. It enables people support to identify training gaps, spot "hidden" competencies (especially relevant with older employees who have acquired skills in previous jobs but may currently be employed on less complex tasks) and carry out succession planning. Some organisations, such as Tesco, have developed a bespoke system of segmentation to describe their staff like that used to profile their customers.[9]

An in-depth knowledge of the employees helps people support to ensure that its activities and policies serve as closely as possible the organisation's purpose. However, in a global survey in 2013, KPMG found that only 15 per cent of managers said that their people-support function excelled at "providing insightful and predictive workforce analytics",[10] and in a survey conducted by Deloitte in 2016, only 17 per cent of HR teams reported that they have a very good understanding of their company's products and profit models.[11]

The extent of internal alignment, management, and impact
(AMI Functional Value Framework, 2016 People in Flow)

---

[8] Sparrow et al, "Do We Need HR?", *HR Magazine* (2015).
[9] Sparrow et al, "Do We Need HR?", *HR Magazine* (2015).
[10] KPMG and the Economist Intelligence Unit, *Rethinking Human Resources in a Changing World* (2013).
[11] Deloitte, *Global Human Capital Trends 2016*.

In bringing this concept to life, there is a need to get back to our initial statement: everything must align with the achievement of purpose and intent. The required attributes, objectives, actions, and results required at all four levels (individual, team, function, and organisation) will flow from the purpose and intent and then flow back to them in implementation. This then makes management of priorities, measurement, and reporting of impact relatively straightforward.

On initial completion, these can be incredibly complex and may contain many lines. Detachment can occur easily when this happens, and so in the process of alignment is also the sub-process of simplification. People Support teams including (OD) and learning and development (L&D) are all guilty at times of overcomplication. This process of simplification is helpful to all and can energise all involved.

There must be a contribution expected of every role, that which the employee is being paid to deliver, that which the employee is really obliged to provide to those paying. Keeping the purpose of the organisation in mind at every step, how can each role contribute to performance? How can the clarity of role expectation be given, and what role do traditional job descriptions and role profiles have? The "points for grade" concept has created a mini cottage industry in wordsmithing. What are the alternatives? How can you determine fairness and flexibility?

Complication is often caused by this "need" to classify a job or role, to give it a hierarchical level, and to generate a managed pay range. By determining the potential contribution, value, skill set, and depth needed to achieve in this way, you are naturally arriving at a value. If you can be comfortable with what the market decides, and you take money off the table in the way Dan Pink describes within his book *Drive*, then simplicity and clear direction can be enabled. This, being the purpose of our functions, should be our aim. Expertise can create simplicity that works. Let's go beyond complication.

We utilise the following 'Intended Impact Grids' based on the work of Robert Brinkerhoff in his 'Success Case' model (Impact Maps). This helps to define and clarify the process of alignment and ensures every role is ultimately contributing to the achievement of organisation purpose and intent.

Where are the pressure points, the areas in the structure of an organisation where action can have a real impact on organisational performance? What are the market levers; where is this likely to impact on or demand more of people? When developed logically, the answers to these questions provide opportunities to see links across organisations, to explore overlaps in output, to streamline and focus individual intent, and to enable people to deliver with strengths in a coordinated and collaborative way. The grids begin the process of informing and should not be "secret". The open sharing of expected contribution enables energy, focus, and the identification of duplication.

Trust and flow are both key to the alignment of every aspect of the organisation. When these are in place, then stress is dramatically reduced, as are costs. Stephen M. R. Covey relates to the trust and cost elements in his book *The Speed of Trust*. When flow is generated, the effects are multiplied. The commercial sense in reworking the job-sizing approach is evident and can radically change if impact people support is to be achieved.

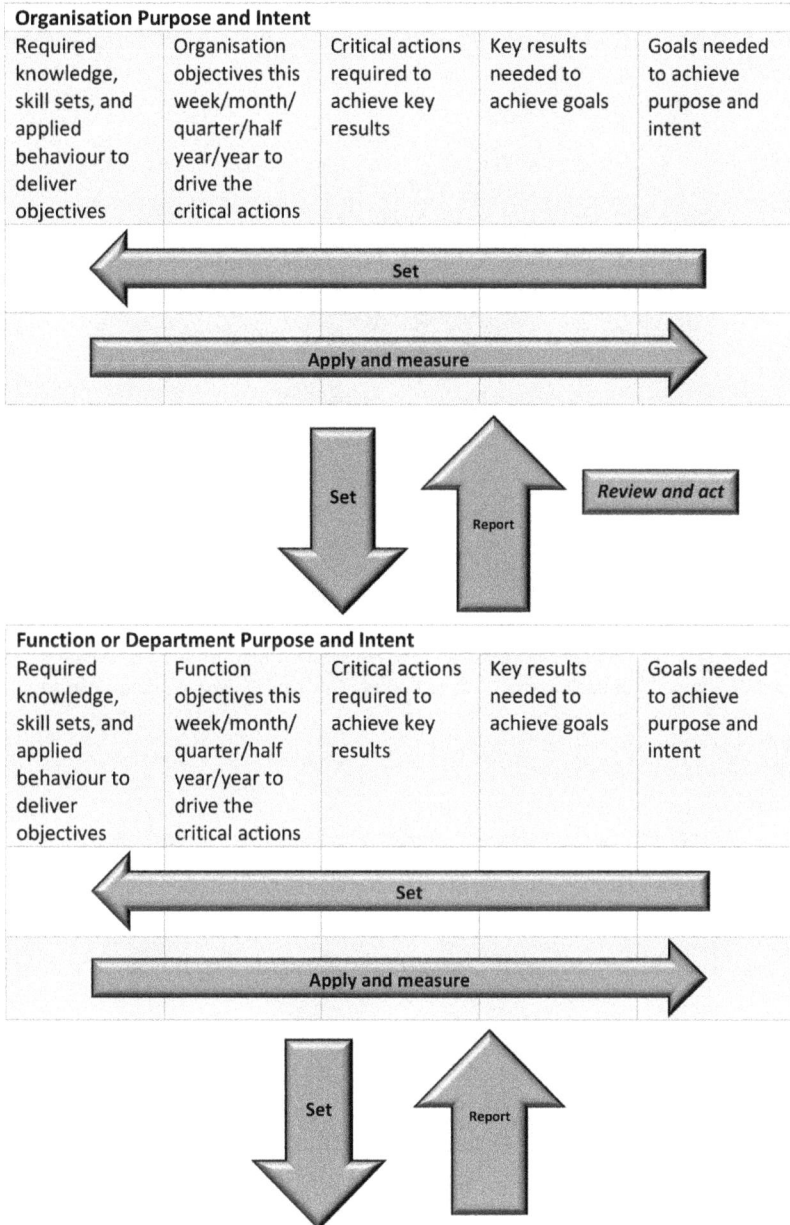

Table 1.1

Organisation Purpose and Intent				
Required knowledge, skill sets, and applied behaviour to deliver objectives	Organisation objectives this week/month/ quarter/half year/year to drive the critical actions	Critical actions required to achieve key results	Key results needed to achieve goals	Goals needed to achieve purpose and intent

← Set

Apply and measure →

Set ↓   Report ↑   *Review and act*

Function or Department Purpose and Intent				
Required knowledge, skill sets, and applied behaviour to deliver objectives	Function objectives this week/month/ quarter/half year/year to drive the critical actions	Critical actions required to achieve key results	Key results needed to achieve goals	Goals needed to achieve purpose and intent

← Set

Apply and measure →

Set ↓   Report ↑

Team Purpose and Intent

Required knowledge, skill sets, and applied behaviour to deliver objectives	Team objectives this week/month/ quarter/half year/year to drive the critical actions	Critical actions required to achieve key results	Key results needed to achieve goals	Goals needed to achieve purpose and intent

← Set

Apply and measure →

Set ↓   Report ↑

Role Purpose and Intent

Required knowledge, skill sets, and applied behaviour to deliver objectives	Individual objectives this week/month/ quarter/ half year/year to drive the critical actions	Critical actions required to achieve key results	Key results needed to achieve goals	Goals needed to achieve purpose and intent

← Set

Apply and measure →

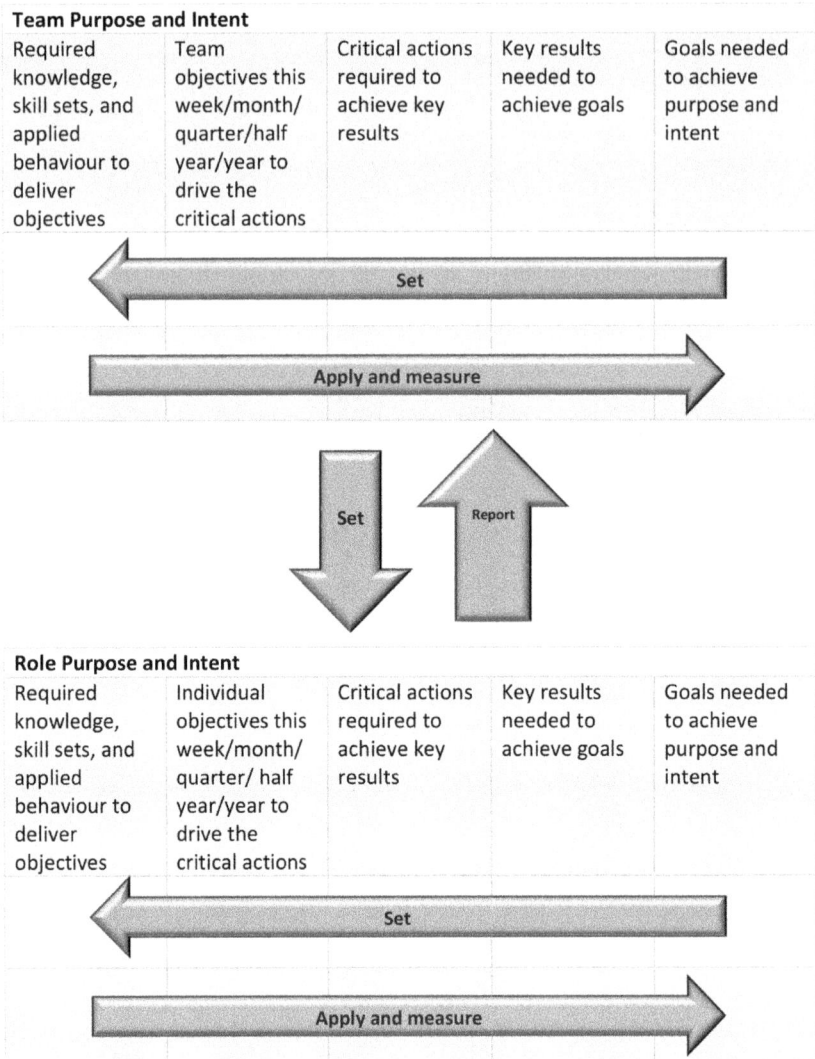

Beyond alignment is the extent to which people support processes and technology are truly integrated within other business priorities, how much they enhance, and how little they delay. The extent of internal management focus on analysis, efficiencies, credibility, wider industry and global consciousness or awareness, effectiveness, and sustained impact are all also key in the recognition of ensuring a focus on what matters.

The points above link to Operational Excellence and Functional Mastery. Credibility comes from reporting the right things to the right people in the right way at the right time. Understanding the needs of other managers will open channels of contribution for people-support teams. This creates a chance to make a real difference and be deferred to in implementing change. People support teams are notoriously akin to the cobbler's shoes analogy in that they are often underfunding their own development for fear of perceived weakness in doing so, or perceived waste. Being as good as possible enables greater innovation. Just do it appropriately. Linked with the potential perceived value is communication.

How to communicate with the rest of the organisation—talk the right talk

Like any other specialisation, HR, or people support, has developed its own jargon and terminology. Unfortunately, these terms are seldom understood by those working elsewhere in the organisation, and this merely serves to isolate people support professionals from everyone else. People support must speak the language of the organisation, not the language of the HR manual. There are many good examples of HR teams who are getting it right, however, even then there is room to increase acceptance of impact.

The chief operating officer of a major bank was heard to say: "Talent development, training, learning and development, leadership and management development, new managers' development, graduate development, organisation development. To people in other departments, what is the difference? Isn't it all related?"

This is a perfect example of the way in which people support professionals, through their relentless use of HR-speak, often succeed in isolating themselves from their colleagues in other departments, giving the impression that they (people support) are working in a silo, which has little if any relevance to, or crossover with, the rest of the business. One of the authors had a meeting with a local council. In it, three people appeared to be effectively doing the same job. Each had a different agenda, focus, and view of priority, and all were led by their perception of what "good" looked like. Commercial mindsets and language matter. "Commercial" needs more than "do it myself" or "we don't do the boring bits"; it means working through with business where value is added and can be further added. "Language" means to speak the language of the business so that you are in tune with the rest of the organisation.

"HR must develop a deep understanding of the business—in the same way, and using the same 'language', as other managers."[12]

Learning and development is the area of people support work which has the most frequent and direct contact with others in an organisation. The conclusions of the 2015 CIPD Learning and Development Survey state: "L&D needs to actively promote its value and credibility by speaking the language of the business."[13] One of the interviewees who was asked for reflections on the survey's findings made the link between the language used by L&D on the one hand and the perception of the function's alignment with the business on the other: "Getting senior sponsors and line managers to think differently about the purpose of L&D is critical in ensuring there is clear business alignment—but L&D also needs to speak the language of the business and demonstrate commerciality."[14]

The failure to use the language of the business merely serves to reinforce the impression held by many that people support is operating in an environment which is somehow separate from the rest of the organisation. What we need is both more straight talking, and the use

---

[12] KPMG, *Rethinking Human Resources*.

[13] Chartered Institute of Personnel and Development, *Learning and Development*, annual survey report (2015), https://www.cipd.co.uk/Images/learning-development_2015_tcm18-11298.pdf, with the permission of the publisher, the Chartered Institute of Personnel and Development (www.cipd.co.uk).

[14] Ibid, 36.

of language which shows that people support professionals understand what the business is all about, and how their work can affect it.

Between us, the authors can speak English, French, and Spanish. If anyone speaks to us in any other language, we're lost. Luckily for us, and for all the other English speakers who don't understand Swedish, many Swedes speak English.

If we meet one of the huge number of English-speaking Swedes, he or she will be able to speak to us in our own language, and we will understand one another. The very thing they are *not* likely to do is speak to the two of us in Swedish and expect us to understand. *They* would be perfectly at home speaking Swedish, obviously, but they would realise that it means nothing to us.

People support professionals can speak the language of those they work with, but all too often they choose instead to speak their own version of Swedish (i.e. HR-speak, a language spoken by very few other than its originators), even though a perfectly good alternative is available which would be understood by all.

Let's admit an unpalatable truth here. For people outside the people support function, some of the language used by people support professionals isn't just a turnoff; it is also a source of amusement—a joke. The authors are passionate about the need for the people support function to improve the way it communicates with everyone else, and at the same time improve its standing in the eyes of others. People support professionals are immensely skilled at coming up with good ideas and then shrouding them in so much jargon and verbal froth that no one else knows what we are talking about. How many good ideas have been ignored simply because HR professionals failed to describe them clearly and made them sound like some outlandish, quirky fad, rather than something which could genuinely improve performance?

An obsession with euphemisms, the use of acronyms never seen elsewhere, an aversion to plain English, a wordiness which would be funny in a sitcom but which frequently obscures all meaning— all these things do nothing but undermine the message of any communication and isolate people support from everyone else. HR-speak gives the unfortunate impression that people support professionals work in a silo which has nothing to do with the rest of the organisation, and persist in using their own language, despite knowing that most other people don't understand it.

"HR needs to eliminate the jargon of its specialization (the same challenge IT continues to face) and begin to link its work more explicitly to business value."[15]

"Not in the real world"; "in a world of their own"; "out of touch with the real world"; "candyfloss castle"—all of these expressions, and many more which cannot be repeated in print, are used by non-HR employees to describe the perceived isolation of the people support function from the organisations it is meant to serve. The very language used by people support professionals plays a key role in creating this impression. These jibes should not be dismissed as the words of the unenlightened or considered by people support professionals as some sort of badge of honour showing how difficult their job is. These expressions are a sad indictment of the way in which the HR function has drifted away from both the organisation's purpose and the very employees it exists to support.

If "start with the business" means aligning all people support activity with the organisation's purpose, then it must also encompass aligning our language with our audience. To enhance credibility, don't use HR-speak when speaking to an audience whose first language is plain English.

---

[15] KPMG, *Rethinking Human Resources*.

"L&D needs to actively promote its value and develop its credibility, by speaking the language of the business and outlining how HR contributes to business goals."[16]

The L&D function is particularly vulnerable to this syndrome, and the fondness for dressing simple ideas up in needlessly complex language has for decades been responsible for obscuring the message of valuable training.

Perhaps one of the most off-putting attributes about the execution of HR initiatives is their proclivity to become bogged down with slogans and buzzwords that, rather than energize a company's communication efforts, often obscure meaning and do more to annoy than inform.[17]

Even simple terms such as coaching when referred to as a coaching culture can be off-putting. In this case are we not wishing a 'helping' culture where all are prepared to help others succeed? When we refer to Listening as a competence or capability, is it not simply showing interest or understanding? Perhaps the single most effective measure which people support could use to raise its standing with the rest of the organisation would be to review and completely overhaul its vocabulary, and start speaking the same language as everyone else. Decades of under-appreciation and underselling ourselves could be undone if only we took the trouble to cut out the HR-speak and use plain language.

People support must be aligned to serve the organisation's purpose in all it does. Only then can it be said to be playing a valuable and truly strategic role which will have a genuine impact on the organisation's performance.

---

[16] Chartered Institute of Professional Development, *Learning and Development*. with the permission of the publisher, the Chartered Institute of Personnel and Development, London (www.cipd.co.uk)

[17] Jake Holwerda, *Communicating for Engagement*, 2007.

Achieving this degree of alignment and understanding requires people support professionals to spend time with managers in other areas of the organisation in order to give them an appreciation of their perspective. This will not only help them to gain knowledge of the business, but will also help to counter the widely held misperception of people support operating in a silo, separated from other departments.

Beyond this, and for any change to happen, the positive "me" benefits should also be considered. Things such as more time, reduced stress, greater trust, enhanced flow, greater energy, improved well-being, consistency in behavioural application, and respect all matter to people and are often overlooked in consideration of strategy and its communication.

"HR people like to be called Business Partners but sometimes show little interest in understanding the underlying financial model of their business or organisation. Without this basic knowledge of what drives the operations, how can they expect to support line managers intelligently in the achievement of business goals?"

—Andrew Mayo, Professor of Human Capital Management at Middlesex University[18]

How people support contributes to the organisation's performance

In the 2015 CIPD survey,[19] only 14 per cent of employees thought that their HR department was involved in organisation strategy.

HR should "use fairness and honesty, with a knowledge of the business" (employee comment in the 2015 CIPD survey).

---

[18] Corporate Research Forum, *Developing Commercial Acumen* (2017).

[19] Chartered Institute of Personnel and Development, *Learning and Development*. with the permission of the publisher, the Chartered Institute of Personnel and Development, London (www.cipd.co.uk)

"One way or another, [HR] will have to gain the business acumen needed to help organisations perform at their best" (Ram Charan).[20]

"The strategic HR role focuses on aligning HR strategies and practices with business strategy" (Dave Ulrich).[21]

The Corporate Research Forum report *Developing Commercial Acumen*[22] speaks of the need to establish a clear linkage or "line of sight" between people support activities and business outcomes. Showing such a connection is not always easy, but when it comes to activities such as recruitment or training, it should be possible to show how people support's efforts can be linked to organisation performance. Training in customer service skills, for example, might be shown to be linked to a reduction in customer complaints or an increase in customer satisfaction scores in feedback questionnaires, while revised recruitment procedures might be shown to have helped reduce dropout rates in induction training. In this way People Support can show in practical terms how it adds value to the business.

The evaluation of people support activity, and especially any involving learning and development, is essential to demonstrate people support's impact upon performance. How any people support initiative can be evaluated should be considered *before the activity starts*, and the measures to be used should be developed to ensure that they will be relevant and comprehensible to non-people support managers. Line managers should be involved in designing both the initiative itself and the measures for evaluating it. In a 2015 survey,[23] the involvement of managers in evaluation was shown

---

[20] Charan, Ram, *It's Time to Split HR*, *Harvard Business Review* (2014).

[21] Dave Ulrich, *Human Resource Champions* (Harvard Business School Press, 1997).

[22] Corporate Research Forum, *Developing Commercial Acumen* (2017).

[23] Chartered Institute of Personnel and Development, *Learning and Development*, with the permission of the publisher, the Chartered Institute of Personnel and Development, (www.cipd.co.uk)

to be more likely in organisations in which L&D showed a greater alignment with business strategy.

L&D activities offer opportunities to show a direct connection with the core of the business. The extent to which employees can transfer their learning into the workplace is an indication of the value to the business of any training initiative, and thus a perfect opportunity for the wider people support function to demonstrate its value to the organisation. However, this opportunity is being missed in many organisations. In a 2015 survey of learning and development in the UK, the CIPD found that less than a third of organisations overall[24] measured the impact of L&D events on productivity. Manufacturing and production led the way in this field, with a hardly stratospheric 35 per cent.

Imagine that you are managing a production line. When you send employees off on a course, or allow them time to undertake online training, wouldn't you be quite keen to know whether the time spent on this was worthwhile? If they work on an assembly line, for example, wouldn't you like to know whether their training has made any difference to the way they do their work? Unfortunately, only an exclusive minority of such managers (the lucky 35 per cent in the case of manufacturing) can answer these questions, because an overwhelming majority of organisations simply don't bother to find out.

Providing managers with information on the transfer of learning and its effect on employee productivity would simultaneously give a clear measure of the success of training initiatives and show L&D (and by extension people support as a whole) directly serving the core aims of the organisation.

In conclusion, it is an unwelcome truth that people support will never be viewed as anything but an ivory tower until members of

---

[24] 29 per cent; ibid.

the profession accept the challenge of becoming wholly aligned with the core purpose of their organisation. People support professionals must understand the key areas of the business, preferably by spending time in those areas and gaining a first-hand knowledge of the day-to-day work performed by the employees. We must ensure that we take every opportunity to show exactly how people support contributes to the business, but to do that, we must first understand the business ourselves.

Showing that people support professionals inhabit the real world, and not some parallel universe which has little or no connection with the one where business is done, will begin to demonstrate the real value to the organisation of people support's work. But in a world of evidence-based decision-making, that value can only really be shown using hard data, and as a profession we are far from impressive in our use of data.

No one expects people support specialists to suddenly become rocket scientists or professional number crunchers but developing the capacity to present and understand basic data relating to people support performance will enable the profession to quantify where possible the results of our work, to stand on equal terms with other specialisations such as marketing and sales, and to exert appropriate influence at board level.

The evaluation of people support initiatives, and especially L&D activity, has always been a thorny issue. It's often something which no one thinks about until halfway through a project, and even then, it's odds on that some of the data needed for evaluation have not been recorded. Evaluation is all part of demonstrating the value of people support, and it should be designed in from the beginning. The failure to evaluate takes us back again to people support professionals' aversion to using data to show the value of their work.

It is not enough for us as a profession to be convinced of the value of our work. We must prove it to others, especially at board level, if we are to gain the respect and influence we deserve. The solution is largely in our own hands.

How people support could contribute more

Taking the lead in the establishment, generation, and maintenance of the organisation's spirit would be a major leap. What is said by leaders needs to be continually reinforced by the way in which the spirit, as well as the output, is enabled. If people are the most important asset, then let that be so. Treat them and be with them accordingly.

When implementing change, community awareness is also a strength that all within people support could further develop. The key influencers within organisation subcultures or communities have a significant impact. CX-Ray is a company who have developed an application that helps to map social networks within companies.

To take on the challenge of building trust and enabling flow, to reduce stress (not necessarily pressure), and to let people perform are the subtexts of any people-related strategy. Helping to overcome the issues of status, process, secrecy, commitment, and context will help.

The collective feel needed to achieve as an organisation

The spirit we referred to earlier is born of an ability to relate to the organisation's purpose. Helping to create a collective "feel" demands going beyond data and getting inside the ways in which individuals relate to the vision, what is being said, and what is being felt now, and then foreseeing what each needs to be if performance intent and purpose is to be achieved.

Where do the feeling components have an impact?

Figure 1.1 **Unity in achievement.**

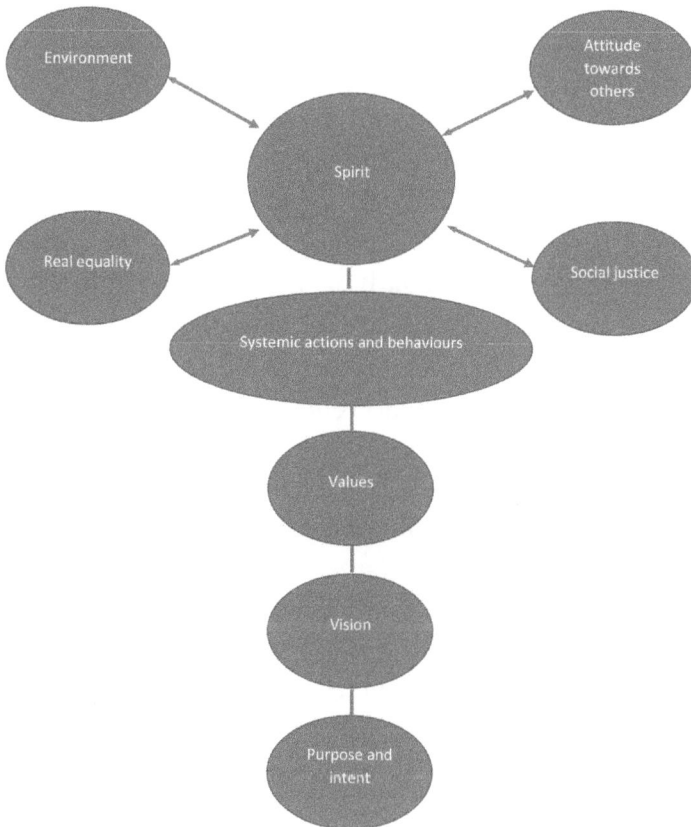

The objectives, actions and results required at all four levels

Individual, team, function, and organisation levels and their alignment are looked at in more detail later in *Go Beyond*, but suffice to say that there are many ways in which these can be used, and it is time to consider how best this is done in your own organisation. The need for clarity of role in every context is key to success and the historic v. future needs and responsibility conundrums will need to be addressed. The what-if scenarios are often helpful when seeking to gain commitment.

The expected contribution of every role

As noted, the expected contribution of every role is key and is often managed more easily when going beyond job titles.

Job titles can often be a drawback, and the size of any challenge can often be measured by the open use of job titles in the way people introduce themselves. This can range from the Christian name only—easy to gain acceptance to the full name—to the surname (starting to see barriers ahead), to the surname and title, to the title only (ego and territorial barriers ahead), to the new extreme, the self-appointed kingdom only as given to one of the authors by a cricket administrator who referred to himself as Mr (county name) ... (potential dictatorship!)

Where time can be created to enable focus

A recent visit to Scandinavia demonstrated just how much can be achieved when things are cut back to what really matters and people respect the time of others. It isn't the role of people support to set out to design roles that cannot be achieved within the paid time. It is, as seen in Denmark and Sweden, possible to have fewer meetings, shorter meetings, open communication, and trust levels that create time, reduce costs, and enable real expertise to play. Just a thought ...

Where the levers of performance are

Where will value be added in any process in terms of the contribution to the achievement of purpose? When do meetings really add value? When considering these, make the area of consideration wider to identify where impact can be enhanced.

What matters most to the people within the organisation

An understanding of this can open an array of opportunity. An appreciation of related contributory influences such as dominant energies in different parts of the organisation and how these provide impact will all add to the potential to implement change effectively.

Going beyond standard data is not easy, but when in possession of the deeper insights, the resulting simplicity can significantly impact achievement and costs.

Operational Excellence

Operational excellence is more than just a matter of professional competence. It also reflects the ability to align all the people support activities in an organisation, including the whole range of learning and development (conventional courses, one-to-one coaching, mentoring, action learning, etc.), with the organisation's purpose and objectives.

In the 2015 CIPD survey of Learning and Development, only 26 per cent of respondents thought that their HR department excelled at "achieving operational excellence". There is clearly a lot of work to be done!

A few years ago, one of the authors attended a presentation which was designed to outline the arrangements for a major programme of redundancies in a large public-sector organisation. Several hundred people were due to be made redundant in response to spending cuts required by the government.

One of the questions asked at the end of the presentation related to whether a female employee could be made redundant while on maternity leave. The presenter gave his response with confidence, but a week later this was shown to be 100 per cent wrong. In the meantime, several staff had been advised by their line managers based on the original, inaccurate advice. Would you be happy to consult the presenter in the future on any other issues relating to redundancy? Or, indeed, on anything else? What about the department that person represents? Would you feel confident in its professional standards and ability to provide employees with accurate information?

Any failure to deliver the basics undermines confidence in people support/HR in the eyes of the function's customers, the employees, and is also a serious obstacle on the road to recognition as a strategic partner in the business.

"Most HR operations are simply looking at doing what they already do a little better. The front runners recognise the crucial importance of understanding and meeting today's more exacting user expectations. This is leading to a radical rethink of how HR interacts with and supports the business."[25]

Two surveys of businesses worldwide have investigated the future of HR—or, rather, people support.

In 2012, KPMG commissioned the Economist Intelligence Unit to investigate the influences on the development of HR. This resulted in *Rethinking Human Resources in a Changing World*, which set out to predict what HR might look like ten years into the future, and particularly how technology might influence HR's development.

In 2014, PricewaterhouseCoopers (PwC) undertook a global survey of operational excellence in HR, which led to the report *Delivering more for less. What sets top performers apart?*

Both surveys identified the same three key areas for action needed by people support to improve operational excellence:

---

[25] PricewaterhouseCoopers, *Delivering more for less. What sets top performers apart?* (2014).

- improved employee access to HR, particularly with technology
- the use of workforce data to aid decision-making
- the recruitment and retention of the best available talent.

Employee access to people support

An employee's first point of contact with people support is hugely influential in forming his or her opinion of the service overall and, indeed, of the organisation itself. The authors (and, I suspect, many of the readers) can testify to the fact that being kept on hold for several minutes on the telephone, for example, does not improve either our mood or our opinion of the department we are trying to contact. The simpler our enquiry, the more impatient we are likely to be when kept waiting.

The PwC report emphasises that when an organisation's external customers have easy online access to its services, its employees, who are people support's internal customers, are likely to expect similarly easy access to the people support function.

The use of IT to provide employees with their first point of contact for people support ensures that all enquirers receive a uniform service, and that simple queries can be dealt with through lists of frequently asked questions (FAQs), without having to disturb a member of staff with a minor enquiry. It also prevents employees from simply contacting the only person they know in people support, and expecting that individual to refer them to the appropriate person. An electronic first point of contact ensures that the employee is given accurate information and, where appropriate, referred to the right person the first time. Video reinforcement of key messages will also add to a sense of belonging.

The ability of people support to provide access that helps rather than hinders is key. The clunky and perceived additional work created by, for example, many performance management systems, does not add value.

Using workforce data to support decision-making

"The insights that can be gleaned from rigorously collecting and analyzing data, and creating insightful forecasts on the back of it, is a key tool in enabling HR to shape the organisation's people resources to deliver on its underlying corporate strategy."[26]

"Analytics is a business priority, not merely an HR tool."[27]

The use of IT to provide the first point of contact with people support provides a source of data on employees and their enquiries, and allows the collection of feedback on the service from its customers within the organisation. In fact, the topic of customer (i.e. employee) satisfaction with the people support function helps illustrate some of the gaps in existing HR departments' use of data on the workforce. The PwC survey in 2014[28] revealed that 61 per cent of the HR departments surveyed did not include customer satisfaction in any of their service level agreements, and 27 per cent did not measure customer satisfaction at all.

In the 2012 PwC annual Global CEO Survey, respondents said they valued, and wanted more, information on staff productivity, employees' views and needs, and the return on investment in human capital. Often less vital than impact yet still relevant, this is often badly misinterpreted by people support functions. In the 2015 PwC survey, 80 per cent of CEOs described data mining and analysis as strategically important. Sadly, tragically in fact, in a

---

[26] PricewaterhouseCoopers, Annual Global CEO Survey (2015).

[27] Deloitte, *Global Human Capital Trends 2015: Leading in the new world of work*, (Deloitte University Press, 2015).

[28] PricewaterhouseCoopers, *Delivering more for less. What sets top performers apart?*, Price Waterhouse Cooper, (2014).

2012 KPMG survey of business executives,[29] more than half of whom were actually in HR, only 15 per cent of respondents said that their company's HR function excelled at "providing insightful and predictive workforce analytics".

Let's just pause and digest that for a moment. Can there be any clearer illustration of people support's failure to deliver operational excellence, or to align itself with the needs of the business? We have a situation where many CEOs want something, and yet in most cases their people support departments don't provide it. Imagine a company which knows that 80 per cent of its customers want a product or service, but which doesn't meet that demand. Just how long would it stay in business? This whole situation is rendered even more catastrophic by the fact that, in a 2012 survey,[30] 79 per cent of CEOs said that their chief human resources officer reported directly to them. So, the great majority of heads of HR/people support departments are failing to deliver something which their immediate boss needs!

"People analytics, a strategy that has been evolving over the last several years, has the potential to change the way people support will work. However, organizations appear to be slow in developing the capabilities within people support to take advantage of analytics' potential."[31]

Data is actually gathered and reported by most. Often reams of data; just not well considered as to what is relevant and to whom. The perception of the value being provided is not helped when the data is seen as irrelevant or there is a lack of insightful analysis.

Gathering data and providing analysis which enables the CEO and board to make evidence-based strategic decisions would

29 KPMG, *Rethinking Human Resources* (2012).
30 PricewaterhouseCoopers, Annual Global CEO Survey (2012).
31 Deloitte, *Global Human Capital Trends 2015.*

considerably enhance the people support function's standing and give it a voice in determining the future direction of the organisation, making it a true strategic business partner. Conversely, nothing is more likely to undermine people support's reputation, and give others a reason to deny them a place at the top table, than failing to deliver on the strategic requirements of the organisation's senior executives. Equally, what matters to line managers in guiding their impact and actions, what matters internally to people support to enhance their impact, and what matters to employees are all different. Tailor data to recipients.

"HR can carve out a unique role by identifying and interpreting the potential impact of longer term social and demographic trends, such as ageing population, on the organisation's business and workforce."[32]

The PwC survey of HR departments in 2014[33] found that nearly 40 per cent did not measure return on investment on previous initiatives before starting new projects, while only 19 per cent had processes in place to cleanse and quality-assure their data to ensure reliability.

Once again, let's pause for a moment to consider the significance of that last figure. It means that four out of five people support departments in the survey are dispensing figures which may be inaccurate, so they run the risk of emulating the person in the redundancy anecdote above, i.e. giving advice which is wrong, and thus risking serious damage to their reputation and credibility, not to mention the business itself. If you give your CEO figures which are quoted in public and which are later shown to be inaccurate, perhaps forcing him or her to apologise, don't expect to be invited to take part in strategic decision-making anytime soon!

---

[32] Corporate Research Forum, *Developing Commercial Acumen* (2017)

[33] PricewaterhouseCoopers, *Delivering more for less* (2014).

"The data collected by HR can provide invaluable information on performance, deployment and recruitment needs. Alongside user-friendly service, the ability to collect, collate and communicate this information effectively is a crucial yardstick against which HR operations are judged by the business."[34]

"The insight that can be gleaned from rigorously collecting and analysing data, and creating insightful forecasts on the back of it, is a key tool in enabling HR to shape the organisation's people resources to deliver on its underlying corporate strategy."[35]

Deloitte's *Global Human Capital Trends 2016* shows HR improving in its efforts to use people data in predictive analysis, although the improvement is a slow one. Globally, 77 per cent of organisations in the survey rated people analytics as important, and the percentage of organisations who considered themselves fully capable of developing predictive models doubled between 2015 and 2016—but only from 4 per cent to 8 per cent! This is clearly an uphill struggle, but things are moving in the right direction. Over the same period, the number of organisations describing themselves as "ready" or "somewhat ready" for analytics rose from 24 per cent to 32 per cent.

"In the not-too-distant future, it will become impossible to make any HR decisions without analytics. Indeed, analytics capabilities will be a fundamental requirement for the effective HR business partner."[36]

The uses to which data are being put are increasingly taking people support data analysis from the merely interesting to the genuinely insightful. Financial services companies and banks are using the analysis of data to identify staff with the potential to become a non-compliance risk, while the monitoring of social media sites such as LinkedIn enables companies to identify flight risk among its employees.

---

[34] Ibid.
[35] KPMG, *Rethinking Human Resources* (2012).
[36] Deloitte, *Global Human Capital Trends 2016*.

We can usefully learn from a model used in the world of intelligence analysis to describe the sequence of events involved in making use of data. There, analysts gather intelligence, assess its reliability, fit it together with any other relevant information, decide what it means, and then tell the people who need to make use of that information.

The sequence is:

- collect
- collate
- analyse
- disseminate.

People support professionals are using workforce intelligence, so the basic principle is the same. We need to gather the data, whether that is feedback from employees on whether they can transfer their learning to the workplace, a profile of their skills and experience, or their reasons for leaving. We should then ensure the data are accurate, before adding them to any other data we already have, and carrying out our analysis.

Sometimes, we fail to embark on this process at all, but where we do attempt it, all too often the process stalls after the analysis stage. We do the difficult bit, carrying out the analysis and producing what's known elsewhere as actionable intelligence, but then fail to tell people about it. Whether through a lack of understanding of the usefulness of that information to the business, a lack of confidence in our conclusions, or because we think other people won't be interested, or a combination of all these factors, the process is not completed by communicating our findings and rendering the information actionable by others elsewhere in the business. Instead, we keep the data to ourselves and go on wondering why other people fail to realise how valuable we are.

"Although companies are submerged in data, transforming data into intelligent insight and disseminating the information across the organization is more of a challenge."[37]

The failure to collect and analyse data, or to communicate the results in support of business decision-making, is often particularly apparent in the field of learning and development (L&D).

The Chartered Institute of Personnel and Development's 2015 annual Learning and Development Survey produced some profoundly discouraging results. The survey found that only 21 per cent of organisations questioned[38] measure behaviour change in participants by assessing the transfer of learning into the workplace, and only 7 per cent of organisations (we so wish that were a misprint, but it really was 7 per cent) measure the impact of learning and development activity on the business.[39] This suggests that the great majority (over 90 per cent) are running L&D activities without even attempting to measure whether those activities are making any difference to the business. To add further gloom to the situation, 14 per cent of the survey respondents do not conduct any evaluation of their L&D initiatives at all.

One encouraging sign is that a recent survey of over six hundred L&D professionals worldwide[40] found that 40 per cent of respondents reported that they planned to recruit new members to their team to work on data analytics.

We will have more to say about L&D later.

---

[37] KPMG, *Rethinking Human Resources* (2012).

[38] Out of a total of 541.

[39] Chartered Institute of Personnel and Development, *Learning and Development.*, with the permission of the publisher, the Chartered Institute of Personnel and Development (www.cipd.co.uk).

[40] Towards Maturity, *Embracing Change: 2015–16 Annual Benchmark Report* (Nov. 2015), www.towardsmaturity.org/2015benchmark.

Predictive insight

Existing HR teams—people support—all have significant reams of data, much of which is produced in monthly packs of varying relevance to those who receive them. What matters to whom is a vital consideration when framing for impact. To move from valued to valuable, a contribution needs to inform the future as well as explore the past and current situation. For insight to be predictive, it should be deep enough to generate considered analysis. It can energise a forward-thinking and positive culture, or it can feed a negative and blame-centred one.

Two banks demonstrated the two approaches, one with weekly management meetings identifying issues and demanding explanations, and with business partners needing someone to blame in meetings with business leaders. Some of the data were unhelpful in terms of business decisions. Business leaders were being invited to manage the HR team as well as their own part of the business, and the time between meetings and the time needed to gather data meant there was little time left to address the issues. The other bank met monthly, focusing on actions needed to meet or maintain intended performance metrics that supported business achievement, and then meeting the business leaders to discuss how collaborative action could potentially impact results, and agreeing ways of moving forward. Each was managing its own domain to work together. At the time, one had significantly better attrition rates, engagement scores, and retail banking results than the other.

What can be predictive? Re-working employee opinion surveys to explore engagement with deeper related factors such as detachment, culture, resilience, and motivation levels allows for analysis links to promote ways in which all can be improved. Performance management that genuinely enables performance and which directly informs succession and talent management can accelerate action discussion.

Impact—dynamic contribution

When speaking to a senior executive, an HR director commented, "Our training courses are largely a waste of time. They don't seem to have the edge and sense of purpose we need people to have." I also met a newly appointed HR director of a large corporate organisation, a member of the main board, who reflected that it was difficult to get the balance of his personal activity to that which he expected in the new role. Another head of HR repeated this dilemma later.

"One of the biggest contributions to both the relevance of training provision and the management and leadership of HR is to focus on aligned performance and how results relate to purpose—at all levels." At a meeting of best practice organisations, a business manager from the sales team presenting their case study spoke with a passion missing from the people support talent manager later in the joint presentation. An awareness of the business case depth was not picked up in the people support team. Despite the apparent alignment, the lack of depth reduced the impact.

Taking the situations one at a time, let's consider the training course perception. Which of the following statements ring true within your organisation?

- Training is needed to comply with our regulator.
- Training takes too long.
- Trainers couldn't do the job they are training for.
- Training takes a long time to deliver to the users.
- Training is lightweight in its intentions, focussing on minor learning objectives rather than the bigger opportunities.
- Training content is too academic.
- We don't know whether our training is really making an impact.

If any of these statements are at all familiar, then it is time to review the training provisions against some key strategic and operational factors, such as:

- the link with the organisation's purpose;
- the objectives set;
- the alignment of those objectives;
- the extent to which performance and results are central to activity balance and design;
- the extent to which individual needs can be accommodated within the range of possible learning options provided; and
- the commercial sense applied within analysis, design, and supply.

Having reviewed over a thousand public offerings and internal training programmes, we have found that stated learning objectives are rarely compelling. It is difficult to appreciate why L&D functions and training companies undervalue themselves so publicly. Very few people will jump for glee over being told that after three days they will be able to list, explain, describe, understand, navigate, etc. These objectives may make sense in terms of guiding a trainer, but they are lazy when used for the learner. Learners need to know what will change, how they will impact differently, what can now be done, and why it matters. To really excite, engage, and promote personal responsibility to perform, start with the end in mind—the organisation's purpose!

Example: a hairdressing salon

Purpose: to cheer people up through their enhanced appearance

Result-focused objectives:

- Stylist – individual: provide high-quality style and cut to every customer
- Salon team – team: provide a coordinated and enjoyable experience every visit for every customer

The focus here shifts to the individual and the collective performance guided by management. So, what training would add value? The key results of the team will focus the critical actions of the role and the learning required to achieve the results necessary to meet the objective and contribute to the purpose. Relevant measurement can be tracked back through the logic.

L&D can help realise the context of expectation, contribution, and intent. With a shared sense of purpose, it is a lot easier to ensure that all involved within the learning-to-performance journey realise their roles and take responsibility, rather than blame training if workplace performance doesn't change.[41]

How does this relate to our other scenario, the people support directors? What drives their balance of time and activity? For an executive role to be more strategic, the clarity of purpose must be in place for the organisation.

The dilemma is further complicated in the same way as we examined in exploring objectives for training. What are the objectives of roles? How well does everything align with and enable the achievement of purpose?

What is the line of sight from purpose, through objectives, through key results, through role-critical actions, to balance of activity? If you are in an executive role, what is the best use of your time? How well can you use the talent within the team? What can be let go to ensure each is contributing their most value?

The need for others to contribute becomes unclear. Where organisations are purely managed, rather than led, the danger of executive leaders focusing on management and micro-management of activity is at its most prevalent. The leap from managing to

---

[41] Adapted from the impact maps introduced by Robert Brinkerhoff in *Success Case Method* (2003).

leading needs an element of development, as humans' ability to trust and let go to others' strengths and to spend time in strategic reflection, development, and guidance is not a natural energy for many.

The flow from this level of thinking will impact the flow of performance. Ensure the flow of learning to the workplace and purpose to action. When this flow can happen, impact from an investment and spend on training activity will be reflected in results, the achievement of objectives, and the realisation of purpose. Everything is connected to purpose; it is worth spending time on it.

Thus, if all independent strategies follow this methodology, then the final check is to complete an exhaustive scenario-planning exercise with all the holders of strategy. The final picture becomes clear. The joined-up strategy becomes known and easily applied by all within the organisation. The commitment to purpose is achievable.

Flow—Organisational Energy

The challenge of internal communications

To conclude this section exploring the framing for impact people support, we need to explore the effect and the significance of communication. The ways in which we communicate to all within the rest of the business influence the perception of value being provided by people functions. Are we telling, sharing, discussing, advising, influencing, authorising, demanding, nudging, helping, supporting, diagnosing, and/or prescribing? At times, it can be any one of these and more, but how often do we stop to consider the context of "why"? Furthermore, how often do we really consider, for every communication, the needs of the receiving audience, and then work out the best medium mix, message, motivation, and timing to ensure absolute clarity, agreement, and commitment?

It isn't simply perception that is influenced by the words chosen and the language spoken. The 'language of HR' is often baffling. To note just a couple of examples, "onboarding" or "induction". These are words associated with having things done to you, and with rituals, not always pleasant ones. This procedure is meant to be a welcome to your new workplace, environment, colleagues, processes, and expectations, and thus a time to rationalise where and how the new person can add value. Why not simply call it what it is – a welcome? Another example is "Talent management". Does this refer to most of the people, all of the people or just a few particularly gifted people?

How inclusive is all this - really? Your Workplace is Your World, yet we can so easily and unintentionally obscure our message through the language we use.

Do we devote as much time to all our presentations to the board, to peer groups, to other collaborating departments, one-to-one, during team meetings, during group meetings, and during events, real and virtual? Do we prepare fully for video conferencing? With each we have the timing challenge, the interest challenge, the language challenge, and the expected next steps to consider.

The way we communicate has a direct impact on the energy of the organisation on any given day. Over the past five years we have realised the links between internal communication and I-Ching are far greater than we had previously credited. The natural energy cycle and the alignment with dominant business energies are both worthy of consideration. To cut to the chase, we now ensure that for all communication, the following cycle template is completed.

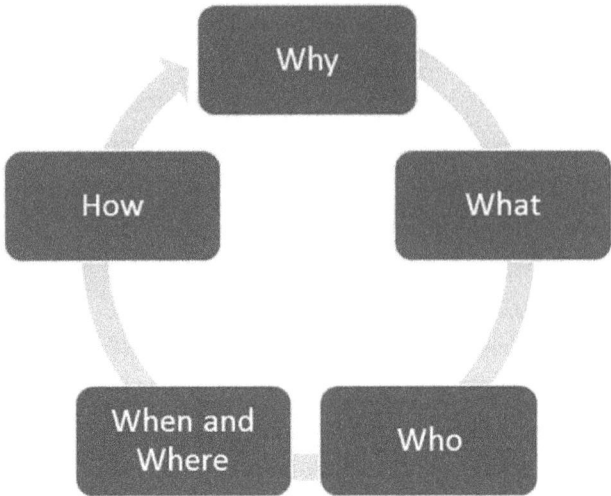

Having established and considered the challenges of interrelated strategies we can now explore the specific functional challenges in more depth in the coming chapters.

CHAPTER 2

ORGANISATION DEVELOPMENT

Recruitment Challenges

Introduction

The fundamentals are well known and easily accessed and acquired. In this chapter we review our findings relating to the challenges facing recruitment as given to us in our survey.

Skills shortage

For years now, recruiters have struggled to cope with the challenge of a shortage of skills among job applicants, and rather than improving as we recover from the effects of the recession, the situation is in fact getting worse. The 2015 Employer Skills Survey found that the number of vacancies in the UK, which were hard to fill because of a lack of skills or experience, had increased by 43 per cent since 2013.[1]

Whilst most people think of this problem purely in terms of a shortage of people with *technical* skills, a lack of sufficient applicants

---

[1] UK Commission for Employment and Skills, Employer Skills Survey 2015 (May 2016).

with a range of people or personal skills is also a major challenge. At establishments in the Employer Skills Survey which reported skill-shortage vacancies,[2] time management was identified as a key personal skill which was lacking in job applicants for 47 per cent of such jobs, while a lack of customer-handling skills affected applicants to 39 per cent of these jobs. Among the technical skills, the lack of IT skills is a challenge (identified as affecting applicants for 22 per cent of skills-shortage vacancies), but this is dwarfed by the lack of a range of complex analytical skills. These include problem-solving skills (affecting applications to 39 per cent of all skill-shortage vacancies) and complex numerical or statistical skills, which affect 29 per cent of such vacancies.

A clear indication of the overall effect is that 66 per cent of employers in the Skills Survey reported that skills gaps were having an impact on their organisation's performance.[3]

The impact of the skills shortage is not limited to headaches for the recruiters. The inability to recruit key staff has the effect of increasing the workload of existing employees. In the 2015 survey mentioned earlier,[4] 52 per cent of employers who had skill-shortage vacancies reported that these led to an increased workload for their staff. This can in turn lead to higher stress levels, sickness absence, and possibly departures of existing staff, thus completing a vicious circle by creating even more recruitment problems. Carrying vacancies can also lead to a loss of business to competitors, difficulties in introducing new working practices, and delays to new products or services. All these effects can be particularly pronounced in smaller organisations.

Laura Braithwaite, HR practitioner at Cassons, accountants in north-west England, reaffirms the skills challenge, quoting her main

---

[2] A total of 3,244 establishments.

[3] UK Commission for Employment and Skills, Employer Skills Survey.

[4] Ibid.

current challenge as recruitment. "The lack of suitably qualified staff results in workload pressures, which is my other big issue." The consequences of the resulting workload pressure are many when you explore stress, absence, burnout, illness, productivity, engagement, and client experience. The costs involved can be significant.

We wonder whether the burden is concentrated in HR or spread across the organisation, or a little of both. It is interesting to note that recruitment is increasingly being mentioned in our research as a concern. Is it the qualifications, work ethic, applied skills, or a disconnect from expectations? Are the problems with supply, or cultural expectation, or other factors? The workload pressures are clearly related, although we have also seen that change by embracing what you have in terms of capability to change workflow. This, though, is a big challenge, particularly in partner organisations where patience is not high in the virtues! Not that this is the case in this instance.

The length of the recruitment process itself can also cause problems. The skills shortage has created a candidate's market, where anyone who possesses the required skills has the upper hand. Any delay in the recruitment process can thus lead to the loss of a well-qualified candidate to another organisation with slicker hiring arrangements. Candidates will not tolerate a long series of interviews and tests for one employer if a similar organisation can offer them an answer after a much shorter process.

"There may be nothing that damages corporate recruiting results more than slow hiring."[5]

---

[5] John Sulivan, "The Top 12 Reasons Why Slow Hiring Severely Damages Recruiting and Business Results", *ERE Recruiting Intelligence* (21 Apr. 2014), https://www.eremedia.com/ere/the-top-12-reasons-why-slow-hiring-severely-damages-recruiting-and-business-results/.

Similarly, a protracted recruitment process may give candidates the impression that your organisation is generally slow in its decision-making. The best candidates are likely to be fast decision-makers, and will be put off by this. Even in the absence of another offer, recruitment delays may lead the best candidates to decide that your organisation is simply not for them.

Creative recruitment—going beyond the standard

The key to meeting all challenges is to have fully defined the role. Why will it exist, what are the performance expectations, what is the energy required, what key skills will be required (which may include the ability to learn quickly), who is the current job holder, and where does that person particularly add value? Do we want a "like for like" value-add potential? How will the person align to your subculture? Do you have clear base values? And are you clear on what good looks like for you?

Where will you find the people you need? Once the above are defined, then the sources of talent for any role can be focused upon. Are you looking for apprentices, graduates, experienced managers, competitors, skilled craftsmen, and/or enthusiastic and energised personalities? By defining in this way, you can neutralise other potentially discriminatory or unconscious bias factors. Building on the concept promoted by Jim Collins in his book *Good to Great*, being clear on the role and focus can ensure the right person in the right seat, on the right bus, facing the right way.

Within the authors' company, we have taken to working as a team on vacancies to clarify the role and to then explore potential sources. We then agree on attraction strategies and allocate responsibilities for exploring multiple channels as appropriate. The team continues to address the remaining questions.

What will attract? Depending on how well the person specification has been cross-checked to working norms and needs, it is possible to start considering your attractiveness as a brand, as a company. What are you offering that will motivate? Are you offering the ability to work alone or as part of a team? Are you offering continuous development or a role that repeats itself daily? Are you offering a proposition to the marketplace that has a clear purpose and intent? Are you offering a pay level that enables people to get behind the role and commit to their performance for the sake of the contribution, or are you using bonuses to drive differentiated performance? The answers will determine whom you will attract and when they would likely respond. You can then look at how you enter the market to attract.

What will differentiate you? You need to be clear that you are a unique organisation, different from any other, simply because you have different people. You may have similar technology, systems, processes, operating models, and structures, but your people are different. What is it about your team that will attract what person? How will this person add value? Will he or she be allowed to?

Who needs to be involved? Where is the value of expertise, insight and the involvement of those with whom a new person will work? Centralised and automated systems such as the "Moneyball" approach taken in baseball seem to have invaded the recruitment world. In baseball it almost worked once yet seems to have been almost blindly adopted by wider sports teams and businesses — most often unsuccessfully. The model is attractive to the efficiency-driven teams. There are, though, too many variables with human performance and situational significant factors. In many roles, particularly in high-volume roles with high attrition, posts should be filled through big assessment centres run by HR recruitment teams or even outsourced organisations. Service-level agreements abound with data on numbers filled, time to recruit, and cost to recruit. It is time to rethink. Add the attrition rates into the calculations.

Managers have a key role with people but are so often given a minimal role in putting the team together. Clarity in the expectations of managers is vital. If they are really players with additional expectations, then who is the person who gets the team to "play" and perform at their optimum? Whoever they are, this person should be involved.

How do you minimise the disruption of the leaver? By involving the team in the replacement, the team is almost accepting the responsibility for ensuring that the contribution of the new player will be welcomed and enabled. They can self-manage any disruption of the leaver.

The challenge of management by headcount—does it manage costs? What are the options? Traditionally these include the use of associates, the use of "on demand resource", "zero hours", etc. At a more senior level, what are the risks? Can the risks be shared or even removed? On the island of Jersey, Simon Nash has introduced the concept of "loan" signings. Essentially, he employs the individual to work inside your organisation. Organisations such as MMC Group are building along similar lines. But how does this help with the headcount management challenge and the hidden variable costs? The owner company has assessed standards, values and cultural fit and takes the risk of employment responsibility. The loaned to company has access to qualified and considered resource as needed, when needed without recruitment costs. The employee will be 'in flow' bringing strengths into organisations as needed.

Many of the challenges relate to the management of expectation and the gap between the expectations of the employer and those of the potential employee. The concept of "bank" staff is not new. You benefit from variable cost management and people as and when workflow demands are high. However, are costs lower when premiums are being paid? If resourcing permanent staff, it is important to manage expectations of *all* involved from the outset, that being the initial interview.

The impact of automated searches

Automated recruiting continues to be a controversial topic throughout the business world. On the one hand, it frees up valuable time for people support workers and provides more useful feedback on candidates' qualifications. However, on the flip side of this, others have suggested that technology has killed recruiting in the way that technology has made the process harder for the applicant. Selection mechanisms that organisations use are stuck in the past. They are often focused purely on the tasks, duties, and tools the applicant has used rather than on how the individual could add value to the organisation. A new recruiting application based on artificial intelligence created by FirstJob moves this forward. It engages with applicants, asks questions based on job requirements, and provides personalised updates, feedback, and next step suggestions. Called Mya, it can also answer applicants' questions about the company. It has been proven to improve recruiter efficiency by 38 per cent and increase candidate engagement by over 150 per cent. A positive innovation.

However, automated application systems need to go beyond efficiency. The rush to efficiency has potentially impacted effectiveness. The fit with the organisation is difficult to establish from keyword searches, and the skills of the interview still have a place.

The challenges with methodology—recruitment myths and confused legislation

The world of recruitment is often seen by those outside as shrouded in mystery and incredibly complicated. When looking from the wider business perspective, this is very often the case. Does it need to be? It is also accused of forever adding to the roles of managers, even though systems are in place to make things easier. Is that true? It depends. Who needs whom in relation to recruitment? Who has the skill set to identify the right people for their team? Who ensures that recruitment is fair and equitable and seeks value from any form of difference?

The distribution of labour through this process is one which is sometimes muddled, although it should be driven by the recruiting part of the organisation. Role profiles, job descriptions, interview templates, and records can all be overly engineered. The simpler they are for all, the easier it is to relate to them.

Despite it being relatively obvious that the simpler the recruitment process, the easier it is for business and the more favourably the business is looked upon, the process still seems to be constantly overcomplicated.

There is a need for simplicity. In this, we would include the need to review whether you *need* to use psychometrics, competence-based interviewing, techniques such as top-slicing, and other methods. All may have a place, but be clear on what value are they adding to the process and the experience. How many interviews are needed before you start to become unattractive as an organisation? Are you reflecting bureaucracy that you don't want, or is it what you want? The answer is yours alone, and thus any approach can be right if it is really what you want to be.

One element of this is the issue of industry experience already referred to. Requiring an individual to have experience in a field when it is not necessary is a deterrent to many more-than-capable people. Consequently, the pool of applicants and the quality of the future employee is limited.

Removing blinkers

Not all roles require experience, and not all roles require *industry* experience. Consider roles that are in themselves a sub-industry, roles that have their own professional standards and institutes or associations, for example strength and conditioning, HR, accounting and finance, legal, IT, marketing, digital utilisation, project management, essential procurement, even management.

Having reviewed a range of vacancies for HR and learning and development (L&D) roles, 45 per cent still require industry experience for roles for which, if recruiting talent, then it is an unnecessary requirement. A genuine expert in people, reward, or learning can quickly learn the industry and the challenges to that organisation, and bring expertise into play. Is your organisation wanting expertise or someone to do as they are told by industry experts who may not be the best in orchestrating people-related support frameworks?

Consider the value that expertise from specialist consulting teams can bring across a range of industries. If you need someone to lead people support functions, then let them lead. When working in a company dedicated to health and well-being, one of the authors has one regret: that the regional sales directors had the final decision in the recruitment of a new type of trainer to deliver new and more impactful training and learning support following a major review. In that process the best person by a long way was ignored, and despite one of the authors flagging it, the sales directors went with a less capable person who would do as they wanted rather than what was needed. The new approach, without the best people, was never going to succeed. Its intent was to change the market and the way the business was perceived. In this case, the head of learning was simply the chief administrator. This undervalued the potential impact and minimised the chances of a new approach, and the result was a return to the old way. Business results remained where they were and fell with new fast-moving competitors entering the market.

Getting the people you need who have your passion and fit your culture

The challenges of finding those you are really searching for starts with a clear definition of *exactly* who that would be in terms of their fit with culture, their skill set, their value alignment, their sense of purpose, credibility, knowledge, and energy.

Given that this is well defined, why the difficulty? We have covered some factors above, yet one is continually self-inflicted. HR has become, not always the guardians of correctness, but often the belligerent. In July 2017, the Tea House Theatre in London advertised a third time for a role. In their advertisement, they quite definitely bemoaned the millennials who had previously applied and the traits they displayed, and were also very clear on what they wanted. They didn't spare the language. The HR world was outraged, with experts everywhere criticising on every forum possible that this was just "not on". The Tea House Theatre was essentially forced to remove the advertisement. Yet, what had they really done wrong? "Experts" on the Chartered Institute of Personnel and Development (CIPD) website stated that the theatre "would miss good candidates with such an ad". Really? We felt that they were helping everyone with absolute clarity and thus would rather attract *only* those who would fit them—and it is their job after all, and their money that will pay them.

There are times when it is not helpful to be too precious. This is a theme that we will continue to reference as we look at the future.

The challenge of Brexit in the UK—an example of global political change

At the time of writing, the sheer uncertainty about the UK's future arrangements with the European Union may deter non-UK candidates from applying for jobs here. In the light of the skills shortage we have already discussed, recruiters will sometimes have to look far afield for the right candidates, but those from overseas may be less enthusiastic about moving to the UK until they know more about the post-Brexit situation.

Marco Reick, people director at Leon Restaurants, noted in a recent discussion, "Evidently, Brexit will have enormous ramifications for businesses and people support departments." He added that the difficulties caused could significantly impact the way Leon Restaurants provide their current very high levels of service. Put together with the additional costs to achieve what they already do with an enforced apprentice levy, the additional 250,000 jobs created recently across their industry could be lost. The consequences of several different legislation requirements and political decisions could create significant pressure on the industry, particularly on the way they recruit and the level of recruitment.

For the effect of Brexit on recruitment to be minimised, Rita Trehen, former chief human resources officer at Honeywell and AES Corporation, stated, "It is vitally important that staff are kept in the loop and they feel as though the business is still in control of its own future."[6] Specifically in terms of recruitment, this primarily involves the business being in control of its employees' future.

William Sheridan, vice president for international human resources at the National Foreign Trade Council in New York, expressed concern about the implications Brexit will have on businesses' ability to retain talent "in this environment of more global uncertainty and more possible exits from the EU".[7]

---

[6] Beckett Frith, "What Brexit Means for HR", *HR Magazine* (24 June 2016), http://www.hrmagazine.co.uk/article-details/what-brexit-means-for-hr.
[7] Andrew McIlvaine, "Brexit: The Human Resource Implications", *HRE Daily* (30 June 2016), http://blog.hreonline.com/2016/06/30/brexit-the-hr-implications/.

This goes back to the idea of control previously mentioned. To retain employees, businesses need to reassure their employees that they are under control despite the "global uncertainty".

The challenge of retention

At a time when it is so difficult to find new people with the right skills, it becomes even more important to hang on to the ones you already have. However, when recruiters are making extra efforts to find those with the right skills, there is a growing likelihood of your best people being lured away to other organisations.

Training existing staff, to provide them with the skills you are seeking from outside the organisation, has the advantage of showing a commitment to people who are already on the inside. It avoids the expense and delay involved in recruiting outsiders, and involves the development of people who are already a known quantity. Any recruitment from outside introduces, by definition, an unknown quantity and therefore involves a degree of risk. Will they fit in? Do they have the skills they claim to have? Will they stay?

Retention is not always a result or sign of an engaged workforce. Take Transport for London, a company that encountered industrial action throughout the first half of 2017 yet had incredibly low levels of attrition or staff turnover. With contracts being offered and paid with higher than average salaries and high annual leave entitlement, post holders would be unlikely, or at least unwise, to leave for purely economic reasons. Whether optimal performance is always achieved is something to ponder. It is something to which deeper insight and analysis would add value when assessing the required attributes and capabilities of those new to the organisation, and once recruited, ensuring those attributes remain to the fore and are utilised well.

Where there is the opposite, that is the costs of recruitment are greatly increased by high levels of attrition, then the causal factors need to be identified and addressed. We have witnessed organisations happily accepting high turnover with the rationale that there will always be high volume. Really? Or are the causes just too difficult and challenging to address? Does people support have the credibility and authority to deal with those factors that are creating the turnover? Could it have been poor recruitment in the first instance, where boxes have been ticked but alignment not explored?

The challenges of the "young recruits"

Let's consider apprenticeships. The UK government introduced the Apprentice Levy in 2017. The authors are concerned about how well the issue was defined and to what extent the "solution" was pre-decided for political impact rather than being a result of thorough consequence consideration. We are yet to have the intent clearly explained beyond the language of straplines. Were apprentices as simply young recruits not being trained previously? Were young people not learning? It is disturbing that an industry that created 250,000-plus of the 1 million jobs claimed by the government is concerned that the levy may mean those jobs disappearing and fewer customer-focused services being introduced. Is the imposition going to backfire? It is too soon to tell, but we are worried that the real issues are not being addressed.

The challenges given to us revolve around the differences in expectation noted earlier. Young recruits bring new skills. They bring high levels of competence in dimensions not fully appreciated by older managers. On the one hand is the issue of incorporation of the skills brought, and on the other hand is the adapting of mindsets to contracts and the world of employment. This remains true for graduates, bursaries, and young talent in any form. They need *experiences* of relevance, and they need to feel they are useful. It is time to rethink the deployment, orientation, depth of learning, and management of young talent, while also bringing some reality to their applied world.

And finally, what impact do these challenges have on your strategy?

Again, we use the natural cycle of energy to ensure we fully resolve need, and prepare and implement the right approach to recruitment for the situation. Ensure the right people are involved to ensure success.

Recruitment and selection strategy template questions

From the exploration of the challenges, we return to the team-focused exploration of strategies for specific needs and the need to address the role questions to determine your actions.

Why?	
What expectations of the values and culture fit do we have?	
What are the key skills needed?	
What energy and passion is needed?	
What can the best do?	
What priorities need to be addressed, and when?	
Who are we looking for?	
Where will we find them?	
When/where will they add most value?	

How would they work?
   a. With whom?
   b. For whom?	

Summary

The challenges of recruitment are many. The consistent theme, though, is the "taking of responsibility by *all* involved for ensuring the right person in the right seat".[8] We would add, making sure they are facing the right way, with the right tools and the right support, and doing the right things for the right reasons.

Keeping People Engaged

What exactly is engagement? Much of the literature on the subject is devoted merely to defining it; it seems easier to spot its results than to describe exactly what it is. A government-sponsored initiative in the UK in 2009[9] unearthed over fifty definitions, so firstly we need a single, clear definition to work with.

This definition, from the Institute of Employment Studies (IES) in the UK, covers the key aspects we want to emphasise: "a positive attitude held by the employee towards the organisation and its values. An engaged employee is aware of the business context, and works with colleagues to improve performance within the job for the benefit of the organisation. The organisation must work to develop and nurture engagement, which requires a two-way relationship between employee and employer."[10]

This definition is important because it emphasises the need for positive attitudes, an awareness of the bigger picture, and a focus on the benefit to the organisation. It also stresses the two-way nature of engagement, calling for commitment from the employer/manager, as well as from the employee.

---

[8] Jim Collins, *Good to Great* (1st edn, Random House Business, 2001).

[9] Department for Business, Energy, and Industrial Strategy, *Engaging for Success: enhancing performance through employee engagement* (2009).

[10] Institute of Employment Studies, *The drivers of employee engagement*, Report No. 408 (2004).

The same IES report identified several behaviours demonstrated by "engaged" employees. These include:

- a belief in the organisation
- a desire to work to make things better
- an understanding of the business context and the bigger picture
- a willingness to go the extra mile.

To these we would add a feeling of being valued and listened to.

Once again, alignment with the goals of the business is crucial. This demonstrates to even the most sceptical board member that engagement has a tangible effect on organisational performance (see below) and is not simply a feel-good initiative. To which we would add the importance of engagement being a two-way process, one which works top-down, through commitment from management, as well as bottom-up, through the action of employees.

Of the more than seven thousand executives and HR leaders who responded to the Deloitte 2016 Human Capital Trends Survey,[11] 85 per cent rated engagement as "important" or "very important". Clearly, people support is pushing at an open door when raising engagement initiatives at the board level, and involvement in engagement measures for which there is well-established evidence for their effect on the bottom line will show people support directly contributing to the organisation's results.

Employee engagement matters because it can be shown to have a measurable correlation with business performance. In 2006, a Gallup review of almost 24,000 business units compared the financial performance of those in the top and bottom quartiles with the same units' scores for engagement:

---

[11] Deloitte, *Global Human Capital Trends 2016: The new organization: Different by design* (Deloitte University Press, 2016).

- Those scoring in the bottom quartile for engagement averaged 31 to 51 per cent higher employee turnover and 62 per cent more accidents.
- Those in the top quartile for engagement averaged 18 per cent higher productivity and 12 per cent higher profitability.

Many organisations use an employee survey as the first step in developing an engagement strategy. Such surveys can be powerful tools for identifying areas of the organisation which are in need of attention, but there are two vital ingredients. Firstly, there must be a management commitment to the fact that the organisation will take action when problems are identified. Failing to do this can have hugely negative results, because employees will feel they are not being listened to and that any survey of their views is merely a cosmetic box-ticking exercise.

Secondly, good top-down communication is needed, to keep employees informed as to the action being taken in response to their concerns. The "You said ..., we did ..." approach shows employees that their views are being taken seriously. Even better is a programme of involving the employees themselves in the process of resolving the problems they have identified.

One of the authors once worked for a large public-sector organisation which ran an annual employee attitudes survey. All employees were urged to complete the lengthy survey, and the results were duly communicated to all employees, but without any indication of the action (if any) which would be taken in response. People support and line management may well have been taking action designed to address problems identified in the survey, but this was not communicated to employees. Staff were thus left with the impression that completing the survey was just a cosmetic exercise, a complete waste of time, and eventually the response rate declined considerably. This reduced the value of the survey and damaged the overall effort to increase engagement.

The 2009 MacLeod Review[12] identified four "enablers" which are essential components of an employee engagement strategy:

- strong leadership
- line managers who motivate, empower, and support their employees
- "employee voice" throughout the organisation, allowing employees to voice their opinions and involving them in decision-making
- organisational integrity: "What we say is what we do."

More recently, some organisations have taken to using social media to supplement or replace surveys. The use of social media allows feedback to be gathered in real time, avoiding the inevitable time lag between survey and results, and enabling employees to interact with each other during the feedback process, as well as simply responding to questions in a survey.

In a survey conducted in 2017 by Andy Holmes for HR in Flow, (now People in Flow) three-quarters of organisations questioned[13] agreed that "social media is becoming increasingly important to the engagement of our employees."

However, opinion was more divided on the use of social media to promote employee voice, the ability of employees to comment on the way their organisation is run. Fewer than 40 per cent of respondents in the same survey[14] said their organisations saw social media as a way of enabling the voice of the staff to be heard. This is surprising, as the immediacy of social media provides exactly the real-time flow of information which allows organisations to identify not what their employees *felt* about some past initiative, but *how*

[12] Department for Business, Innovation, and Skills, *Engaging for Success* (2009).
[13] Andy Holmes, *Social Media and the Engaged Employee* (HR in Flow, 2017).
[14] Ibid.

they are feeling about today's announcement, while there is still time to act to address any problems.

Neither of the authors would claim to be an expert in the use of social media, but clearly this approach is already familiar to, and in daily use by, many employees out of the workplace. Becoming involved thus becomes a more natural, routine activity for many people. Further research is called for on the use of social media in this respect, to ensure that organisations exploit the full potential offered by this powerful means of communication, while ensuring that employees who are not avid users of Facebook or Twitter are not left behind.

Fully engaged employees act as advocates for their organisations, helping to bolster their brand. Recent developments see younger employees going beyond engagement and needing fulfilment. This relates directly to the motivational need of needing purpose. Time spent in ensuring that all can relate to your ultimate purpose enables a potential for fulfilment, engagement, and optimal performance more often. Conversely, employees who are actively *disengaged* and, beyond this, detached, pose a risk to the organisation. This can lead to an increase in staff turnover, customer complaints, returns, wastage, sickness absence, accidents, and disciplinary cases, with consequent damage to the organisation's reputation.

CIPD surveys in recent years have found that between 35 per cent and 39 per cent of employees in the UK are positively engaged. Other results have included:

- Women tend to be more engaged than men.
- Older workers are more engaged than younger ones.
- Managers are more engaged than non-managers.

Rather than simply noting these details and then moving on, let's pause to consider why some categories of employees appear to be more engaged than others, and why 60 per cent or so of UK employees appear to be either un-engaged or actively disengaged. Clearly, we will never see 100 per cent of employees fully engaged, but something less than 40 per cent does seem a pretty low figure.

We have already pondered at some length the adverse effect of people support seeming to speak a different language to the rest of the population. Is the relatively low level of engagement due, at least in part, to this "language barrier"? Are people support professionals and management in general speaking language *X* to a population who mainly speak *Y*? Are the 35 to 39 per cent therefore principally those who can understand the language of people support? A grand title does not confer the right to adopt language which appears to raise the speaker above the level of us lesser mortals. In fact, the more senior the people support person, the better he or she should be at communicating with the people they support.

The CIPD figures suggest that some people, the 30-odd per cent of employees, get it sufficiently to become engaged with their work to a significant degree, so perhaps there is something about the more-engaged groups which enables them to understand HR-speak. Have older employees, for example, simply heard it all many times before, so they can translate what comes from management/HR into plain language? Do managers understand the language because they have more exposure to such terminology at meetings and conferences, and more contact with those who use it? Or are managers in these organisations perhaps able to communicate with their employees clearly because they have already moved away from the language habitually used by HR?

If the figures for engaged employees have remained fairly steady for several years, as the CIPD surveys suggest, isn't it worth trying something different to try to raise them? Isn't one definition of insanity "doing the same thing over and over again but expecting different results"? That being the case, if we are to improve levels of engagement, we need to reconsider existing employee engagement measures, and be prepared to completely overhaul them in the interest of improving levels of engagement.

A point worth making here is that, even though the survey found managers to be more engaged than non-managers, where a manager has become disengaged, this has a disproportionate effect on others, because a single manager's attitudes can affect a considerable number of employees.

The challenge of clarity of purpose: What goes on in the shed? And what has it got to do with me?

Imagine the scene:

A bitterly cold night on a Royal Air Force airfield in eastern England in the early 1980s, with a hard frost on the ground and thick fog in the air. A major NATO exercise is in progress, and two young airmen, armed with rifles, are standing guard over what appears to be simply a large, unimpressive, and oddly shaped green shed not far from the runway. They have no idea what is inside the shed, but they have been told they must challenge anyone approaching it. They are cold, bored, and wishing they could do something worthwhile as part of the exercise, like their mates, some of whom are guarding the missile store.

Three officers approach, all air traffic controllers on their way to check the contents of the shed. Once identities have been checked, the controllers enter the shed. After a while one of them, the youngest, invites the sentries, one at a time (while the other remains on guard), into the shed to show them what it contains, and to explain the importance of guarding it from anyone who might try to sabotage it.

The "shed" was the backup location for the talk-down radar (precision approach radar, or PAR, for the enthusiasts among you), vital for bringing the base's jet fighters back through the fog. It would be used if the regular radar sets in the control tower were rendered unusable by an enemy attack or a technical failure.

The two young airmen watched spellbound as the controllers used the radar in the shed to guide aircraft back to the airfield in spite of the fog, and the effect was enhanced by the fact that each of the aircraft in question changed from a speck on the radar to the real thing roaring past on the runway only a matter of yards away.

The airmen each thanked the officers profusely for showing them what exactly they were guarding and explaining the significance of their cold, foggy task. The young air traffic controller, many years later, went on to write books designed to convince people of the importance of letting people know how their jobs fit into the bigger picture.

Whether they are sentries, receptionists, cleaners, workers on an assembly line, or any other group of employees, knowledge of the connection between their work and the key objectives of the organisation they work for is likely to have a positive effect on their performance at work.

If you leave employees in the metaphorical cold and fog, unaware of how their work fits into the work of the organisation, they will be less motivated, less productive, less efficient, and less loyal to the organisation. Make sure they know what goes on "in the shed", and its relationship to their own work. The shed is any "black box" environment in which a few specialists in an organisation carry out the glamorous tasks which bring in the big bucks. But they cannot do so without the work done by a much larger body of employees who feel distanced from those in the shed.

Doing this sort of thing is hardly a new idea. In 1918, during the First World War, the Aircraft Production Department of the British Ministry of Munitions ran a programme of shop-floor talks and leaflets explaining to factory workers the actions of the aircraft they were building, in order "to give the worker some appreciation of the importance of his personal contribution towards winning the war".[15] To cement this connection, employees' pay envelopes carried pictures of the aircraft in action. Workers in factories in Britain were thus shown the connection between their work and the overall task of their organisation, in this case, winning the war (shades of the NASA employee with a broom in the 1960s).

If the managers of a century ago, in the midst of a war, were able to devise and deploy methods of helping employees to see the connection between their own individual jobs and the overall objectives of their organisation, why can we not do this more frequently, and more effectively, today? We have infinitely more efficient means of communication at our disposal, and yet, as that CIPD survey showed, more than 60 per cent of employees are still not engaged.

Drivers of engagement

The Institute for Employment Studies identifies seven key drivers of engagement:[16]

- The nature of the employee's work has a clear influence on their level of engagement. It is important to have challenging, creative, and varied work that utilises old and new skills.
- A perception that the work undertaken is important and has a clear purpose and meaning.

---

[15] William Philpott, *Attrition: Fighting the First World War* (Abacus, 2014).
[16] Gemma Robertson-Smith and Carl Markwick, *Employee Engagement: A Review of Current Thinking*, Institute of Employment Studies, Report 469 (2009).

- Having equal opportunities for, and access to, career growth, development, and training opportunities is considered important in enabling employees to engage with the organisation.
- Receiving timely recognition and rewards is a key driver. Salary is important, but more as a disengager than an engager.
- Building good relationships between co-workers is important, especially the relationship between employee and manager. This critical relationship needs to be a reciprocal one of making time for, and listening to, one another.
- Employees may engage in an organisation if they can understand the organisation's values and goals, and how their own role contributes to these.
- Leaders and managers who inspire confidence in individuals, giving them autonomy to make decisions with clear goals and accountability, are perceived as engaging.

It is noticeable that most of these are related to action from line managers. They don't necessarily call for great expense or huge strategic initiatives from top management, so first line managers can make significant strides towards building a more engaged workforce. Providing opportunities for training and development, building good relationships with employees, giving recognition, explaining the purpose of their work, identifying clear goals, all of these are within the remit of line managers, and have been proven to make a real difference in levels of engagement. Good managers work with their people and not simply the process. They get the best from their people by helping them to appreciate their role and how it contributes, where their strengths add value, and how they best work with others.

Managers also have an obligation to act as role models for their teams, embodying and modelling the levels of engagement which they want to see from those who work for them.

To the point relating to opportunities for training and development, we would add the importance of being properly equipped for the work being carried out. By expecting employees to work with inadequate or outdated equipment or facilities, management appears to be sending the signal that the work in question is not really important to the organisation. In that case, why should employees view the work as important, when their managers don't appear to?

The implementation of a set of Total Performance Indicators at Sears Roebuck as long ago as 1992 led to several important conclusions relating to engagement, including "an employee's attitude towards the job and the company had the greatest impact on job performance" and "improvements in employee attitude led to improvements in job-relevant behaviour".[17]

The relationship between an employee and his or her line manager is crucial. The line manager becomes an ambassador or proxy for the organisation, colouring the employee's view of the employer. "Employee engagement is a direct reflection of how employees feel about their relationship with their line manager. The quality of the relationship is the most critical factor in determining whether or not the employee chooses to stay at or leave a job."[18]

Engagement is not something that people support can pursue alone. The involvement of line management is crucial. "Employee engagement is ... something that can't succeed by being managed by HR alone. Certainly, HR has the skills and tools to assist but it

---

[17] Gemma Robertson-Smith and Carl Markwick, *Employee Engagement: A Review of Current Thinking*, Institute of Employment Studies, Report 469 (2009).
[18] Anne-Marie Kontakos, "Seeing Clearly, Employee Engagement and Line of Sight", in *Employee Engagement: What do We Really Know? What Do We Need to Know to Take Action?* (Cornell University's Center for Advanced Human Resource Studies, 2007).

is the line managers who need to know how to engage people."[19] So, to engage employees in general, we first must win over line managers to the cause by showing them the benefits of having engaged staff.

But let's not overlook the impact of the involvement of top management as well. In 1914, at the start of the First World War, Lord Kitchener, the British Secretary of State for War (he of the dramatic recruiting posters), wrote to the workers at a munitions factory in Kent: "I should like all engaged by your company to know that it is fully recognised that they, in carrying out the great work of supplying munitions in war, are doing their duty for King and Country, equally with those who have joined the Army for active service in the field."[20]

By equating the activities of factory workers with those of soldiers at the front, Kitchener was recognising the vital contribution of those who worked behind the scenes, often doing fairly humdrum, repetitive jobs. Recognition of this kind from someone at the very top levels of an organisation, in this case the British government, is a clear statement of the importance of the work and its relationship to overall objectives. Kitchener's letter might almost have been designed to illustrate some of the IES drivers of engagement listed above, and yet it was written a century before the IES compiled its list.

The importance of language needs to be emphasised once more, as efforts at engaging employees which use slogans or buzzwords can be counterproductive. In fact, they can fall utterly flat by provoking amusement rather than engagement. The language used has to be straightforward, clear, and unambiguous, with no gimmickry

---

[19] Mike Johnson, *The New Rules of Engagement* (London: Chartered Institute of Personnel and Development, 2004), with the permission of the publisher, the Chartered Institute of Personnel and Development (www.cipd.co.uk).
[20] Kate Adie, *Fighting on the Home Front: The Legacy of Women in World War One* (Hodder Paperbacks, 2013).

or HR-speak to obscure the message. Even the most imaginative, eye-catching communications with employees will be unsuccessful if unclear language is allowed to cloud the message.

One way of developing engagement is to make employees shareholders in the organisation, like the John Lewis Partnership in the UK. The performance of the company thus becomes an obvious matter of concern to everyone it employs, as it determines the value of the shares they hold and the size of the bonuses they are paid. Clearly, this is not possible in all organisations, including smaller enterprises and the public sector, but if not actually *shareholders*, employees at least need to be made to feel that they are *stakeholders* in the success of the organisation.

"Quite possibly the easiest way to improve the engagement of your company's workforce through internal communication is simply to share as much information as is possible with them."[21]

Once again, telling people "what goes on in the shed" helps them to put their own work into perspective and relate it to the work of the organisation as a whole.

"HR is the Pied Piper of the firm, gaining the employees' trust and commitment."[22]

Communication revisited, continued, and expanded!

In *The New Rules of Engagement*, Mike Johnson emphasises the importance of communication as a means of engaging employees, but he adds that all too often the responsibility for managing it is unclear, with no senior person designated as its champion. With

---

[21] Johnson, *The New Rules of Engagement*, (2004) with the permission of the publisher, the Chartered institute of Personnel and Development (www.cipd. co.uk)
[22] Ibid.

no one influential in the organisation able to push things along, or to remove obstacles, communication can break down. Just as with engagement, having a champion for communications is essential to exert influence at board level.

One of the authors once worked in a medium-sized public-sector organisation which was subject to extensive spending cuts, leading to a programme of redundancies. All the members of an occupational group which would be subject to redundancies were invited to a meeting at which the two managers running the redundancy programme outlined the process to be followed.

One of them emphasised the importance of communication in ensuring the smooth running of the process. She then used the "p" word—she *promised* that she would send an email every Friday to each member of the occupational group at risk, giving the latest news of the process. She also said that she would send an email even when there was no news, just to show that management was being completely open and transparent, and keeping employees right up to date. This was all very promising from the point of view of the employees concerned, as it seemed that someone in management had their hunger for information very firmly in mind and would do everything possible to keep them informed.

That was in April. By mid-October that year, only *one* of the promised weekly emails had appeared, and that was simply to apologise for the non-appearance of any others! The result of all this was more damaging than if no one had even mentioned communication in the first place. In the absence of any news, rumour was rife. Management had broken a very public promise, and if they could break a promise relating to something so easy to accomplish as sending an email once a week, could they be trusted to keep any undertakings relating to more challenging things?

There are two pretty obvious points to emphasise here. Firstly, failure to deliver on a promise is fatal to efforts to create trust. The more difficult the times, the more important trust becomes. Things don't come much more difficult than a time of redundancies, and to lose trust at a time like that is disastrous. You can hardly expect employees who are about to be made redundant to feel engaged with the organisation, but what about those who are left behind? If they have seen a breakdown in both communication and basic trust in their employer, how will they feel about the future? Would you feel committed to an employer who fails to keep promises, or would you look round nervously for an escape route? And if you want to escape but can't, just how engaged would you feel?

Secondly, people have an insatiable need for information, and the more difficult and unsettling the situation, the more pressing that need becomes. In the absence of "official" information, rumour, complete nonsense, and straight untruths will circulate. Once that situation has developed, any attempts at communication from management look defensive and rather suspect.

Moving experiences

When your place of work, the place where you spend so much of your life, is due to move, it can be extremely unsettling. The further away the new location, and the less you know about it, the more concerned you are likely to feel. The way an organisation handles such a situation can have a profound effect on the attitude of the employees affected by the move.

While in a public-sector organisation, one of the authors was a member of a team due to move ten miles to different offices. First supervisors, and then all the employees involved, could visit the new location, so that on the first day in the new office, everyone already knew exactly where they would be sitting, where they could park their cars, where the restaurant was, and all the many separate matters which to an organisation may seem trivial but which to individuals who are going to be spending a third of their lives in that office are very significant.

A move may be prompted by expansion brought on by business success, or it may be quite the opposite, the result of the organisation shrinking in size. Either way, it is a time of huge change for any organisation, and the engagement of the employees involved is essential to the smooth progress of the move.

The challenge of detachment—quitting before leaving

Not providing employees with the basics needed to perform their job, whether that's equipment, premises, raw materials, training, or other resources, is a pretty well guaranteed way to demotivate them and "detach" them from their jobs. Outdated tools, vehicles, or buildings, for example, convey an impression of management indifference, and if the management seem not to care about the work, why should the employees?

Detachment, sometimes referred to as disengagement, has also been described as "quitting before leaving",[23] in the sense that a detached employee's productivity, as well as their emotional attachment to the organisation, may decline to such an extent that they might as well not be present. This phenomenon can involve an individual employee or a group, and the impact on the organisation can be very damaging. The attitudes and behaviours associated with detachment are both infectious and toxic.

Early signs of detachment can include a reduced willingness to take part in activities involving the employee voice, such as an employee or a group becoming less prepared to provide feedback.

---

[23] Burns, Detert, and Chiaburu, "Quitting before leaving: the mediating effects of psychological attachment and detachment on voice," *Journal of Applied Psychology* (July 2008).

Organisations frequently recognise detachment only when an employee announces his or her intention to leave, and even then, the exit processes may fail to delve deeply enough to identify the source and extent of the detachment. Even if the exit processes are the only mechanism which picks up details of an employee's detachment, this can, if recorded and acted upon, at least alert the organisation to the possibility of a more general problem, and perhaps prevent the loss of other employees.

So what?

It is utterly impossible to overstate the importance of communication in the engagement of employees. Between us, the authors have worked in or for many organisations, large and small, private and public sector, over the course of working lives which amount to a combined total of almost eighty years. We have heard employees complain, often justifiably, about all manner of aspects of their working lives, but we have *never*, in any organisation, heard anyone complain about receiving *too much* information from management. The more difficult and worrying the times, the more people want to know about what is going on, and if you don't tell them, the rumour mill will simply make things up to fill the gap. "Fake news" is not a new phenomenon, nor is it confined to the internet. It has always been out there, and it thrives and multiplies when real information is absent.

The redundancy situation related above is a case in point. During a period of public spending cuts, there were few complaints in the organisation in question about the *fact* of job cuts. Most people accepted that they were unavoidable, although obviously undesirable. However, they were incensed at the failure of the organisation to keep them informed of what was happening. Rumours circulated, because the absence of news from management was interpreted as a sign that employees were being kept in the dark about developments, rather than an indication of there being no developments to report. And promising information, and then failing to deliver, just makes things worse. *Tell people what's happening, and if nothing is happening for the moment, tell them so.* Telling people that there are things that you genuinely don't know is not evasiveness; it's honesty. You cannot expect employees to be engaged if the organisation is apparently being dishonest with them.

As we are writing this (May 2017), British Airways is suffering a major IT failure which led to the cancellation of all its flights worldwide. Passengers whose flights had been cancelled or who had been separated from their luggage had the same complaint: that no one was telling them anything. No news is emphatically *not* good news in such a situation. No news is a recipe for angry people who will believe almost any rumour, because they have no real information to go on. The same principle applies to any situation being handled by people support.

As well as keeping people informed during difficult times, such as during a redundancy programme, simply telling people what their organisation is doing (including what goes on in the shed), and explaining how their role contributes to its work, is never wasted effort. The examples above drawn from the First World War show that there is nothing new about this, and yet many in management still seem to be unaware of the power of this very simple, easy-to-implement means of engaging employees.

Knowing that someone very senior in the organisation has noticed your work is a huge encouragement. Douglas Conant, as CEO of Campbell's Soup, sends handwritten notes to congratulate employees on their work not because he is short of things to do to fill his working day, but because he knows that this sort of recognition from the very top of the organisation is an immensely effective method of engagement. Support from the very top provides the bedrock on which line managers can build the engagement of their teams. Conant's notes thanking individual employees for their work serve as a marvellous example of this type of senior management involvement in engagement, sending the message that the work of even the most junior staff is noticed and regarded as important by those at the very top.

In a business world which is dominated by digital communications, it is instructive to see that people still value straightforward face-to-face contact with the people at the top of their organisations. As we will see in the section on employee relations, a survey in the UK in 2016 showed that roadshows with senior managers were regarded as the most effective method of communicating with employees, ahead of all digital methods, including emails, electronic newsletters, and social media.[24]

In terms of the effect upon levels of employee engagement, there is simply no substitute for seeing the people at the top of an organisation in the flesh. It is even more effective if a senior figure is designated as a champion for engagement. This signals to employees that engaging them fully in the work of the organisation is of real importance, and is recognised at the highest level.

Tackling change—the challenges

There are many books on change, change management, change coordination, and the ways in which change should be considered, communicated, and implemented. Two of our favourites are written by John Kotter, *Our Iceberg Is Melting* (with Holger Rathgeber) and *A Sense of Urgency*, the latter of which explores one of the most vital needs in more detail.

---

[24] *State of the Sector: Internal Communication and Employee Engagement*, vol. 9 (Gatehouse, Nov. 2016). Roadshows were regarded as effective by 88 per cent of respondents. No digital methods scored above 78 per cent.

In this context, we simply draw attention to the catalytic role played by all within roles in organisation development, people support, and learning and development (L&D). For any change to work, it must not be implemented at a time of internal turf wars. Strong people support and enablement is needed in any change programme, in any transformative initiative. This is specific to the change intent and situation beyond the day-to-day requirements of our roles, and will indeed change those day-to-day requirements once implemented. It is a time to ensure the absolute role modelling of informed, integrated, collaborative, and coordinated management and action. It is time for impact people support to deliver.

No one gets credit or bonus points if change is unsuccessful. If truly engaged, aligned to purpose and intent, then process and people will achieve the intended change. Key to this is the setting of collaborative objectives, the use of intended impact grids noted earlier in the book, and the planning for success. We have attended meetings in which HR business partners have "instructed" other parties within the change support team that they will not be taking any blame, so *when* the project fails they had better not have been the cause! You know this happens, and you also know it shouldn't. It is the unacceptable face of hidden wiring, a concept essentially introduced by Lynda Gratton in her splendid book *The Shift*.

So, once again we return to the order in which we consider action—why, what, who, when, where, and how. The order is important. So many projects fail simply because the planning moves straight from what to how. By spending extra time to clearly define every component, including the team needed, the flow of action is accelerated and is also more thorough. The people support functions need to unite to ensure that these disciplines are followed and managed. For this to happen, the contribution from those functions has to be viewed as valuable.

Go beyond learning

There are so many challenges within the world of learning and performance, and these are largely internally driven.

"In today's business environment, learning is an essential tool for engaging employees, attracting, and retaining top talent, and developing long-term leadership for the company."[25]

The authors both have considerable experience of delivering face-to-face courses, back in those not too far-off days when that was just about all that was on offer by way of learning and development. How things have changed.

Now, in the same way that many employees expect online access to people support services in general, they also expect to be able to learn online. This includes such methods as through apps, learning at their own pace and when they choose, rather than attending formal courses. According to Bersin by Deloitte, face-to-face instructor-led training accounted for 77 per cent of training hours in the UK in 2009, but had fallen to 32 per cent by 2015, although it remained the most common method of delivery for learning and development.[26]

More than just expecting ease of access, employees increasingly want to be in control of their own learning. The dramatic growth of massive open online courses (MOOCs), many of which are free, and the proliferation of apps of every kind, have opened the door for employees to be able to select their own subjects to study, whenever it suits them, and often on mobile devices, which allow access literally anywhere. The growth in the numbers of people undertaking MOOCs has been significant—approaching 50 million in 2016 according to various vendor data and online sources.

---

[25] Deloitte, *Global Human Capital Trends 2016*.
[26] Bersin by Deloitte, *UK Corporate Learning Factbook 2016: Benchmarks, Trends, and Analysis of the UK Training* Market (Deloitte Consulting LLP, 2016).

The more employees experience these advances outside work, the more they come to expect something similar in the workplace.

Employees are increasingly aware that acquiring new skills is the route to advancement at work. As Josh Bersin puts it: " ....in today's economy 'The Learning Curve is the Earning Curve.' Today our skills drive our earnings."[27] Organisations with good learning opportunities are thus attractive to jobseekers, and when recruiting talent is as challenging as it is today, providing these opportunities can be crucial in getting the right people and keeping them. L&D professionals are thus performing a key role in their organisations' talent management efforts, helping to attract and retain top-performing personnel.

"Mobile, social, and web-based platforms that can deliver on-demand learning content are 'must-have' capabilities."[28]

Employees increasingly want to be "in charge", able to decide when, where, and what to study. A survey of 1,600 employees in 55 countries[29] in 2015 revealed that 88 per cent wanted to be able to learn at their own pace, and 42 per cent wanted to be able to do so at weekends or in the evenings, i.e. not on traditional face-to-face courses. However, the same survey, which also questioned 600 L&D professionals, showed that 55 per cent of training was still being delivered entirely face-to-face, with only 26 per cent of respondents saying that their organisations offered blended learning, containing an element of online learning.

But the tide is turning. In another survey of almost 2,000 individuals in the UK, commissioned by the Chartered Institute of Personnel

---

[27] Ibid.

[28] Deloitte, *Global Human Capital Trends 2016*.

[29] Towards Maturity, *Embracing Change 2015–16: Improving Performance of Business, Individuals, and the L&D Team*, benchmarking report (Nov. 2015).

and Development (CIPD) in 2015,[30] online learning was identified as one of the most frequently used learning methods, while 59 per cent of respondents expected their organisations to increase the use of e-learning generally in the next two years. However, online and mobile learning were also identified in this survey as among the *least effective* learning methods.

While we are sure that this does not indicate that employees in the UK are somehow less receptive than others to online learning, or less competent in its use, it may indicate that their experience of learning technologies so far has involved some poor-quality material, which is an important lesson for providers. This may also be linked to the fact that, again based on UK data,[31] many L&D professionals lack confidence in their ability to harness learning technologies in their programmes. Only a quarter of the L&D professionals surveyed described themselves as either "extremely" or "very" confident in their ability to harness technology to enhance their L&D interventions, while a third said they were either "not very confident" or "not at all confident"[32] of their ability to do so.

This lack of confidence appears easy to address. Respondents to the CIPD's UK survey cite such things as "simple terminology" and "more basic courses, guides, or articles" as measures which would help them to gain confidence in using learning technologies, so the L&D profession has a pretty clear steer as to how to improve its performance in this area.

---

[30] Chartered Institute of Personnel and Development, *Employee Outlook* (Autumn 2016), with the permission of the publisher, the Chartered Institute of Personnel and Development https://www.cipd.co.uk/Images/employee-outlook_2016-autumn_tcm18-16797.pdf,

[31] Chartered Institute of Personnel and Development, *Learning and Development*, annual survey report (2015), with the permission of the publisher, the Chartered Institute of Personnel and Development https://www.cipd.co.uk/Images/learning-development_2015_tcm18-11298.pdf,.

[32] 24 per cent and 32 per cent respectively.

However, we must not lose sight of the fact that individuals have different learning preferences, and that not everyone responds well to e-learning methods. Similarly, not all subjects lend themselves to these methods. We need to adopt a "horses for courses" approach, being conscious of the need to cater for a range of individual preferences and the best fit between topic and method.

Nevertheless, most organisations appear to be using learning technologies[33] to some extent, with three-quarters in the UK survey using such methods, and 88 per cent of those in the public sector.[34] But more traditional methods still dominate. Of the organisations using learning technologies, two-thirds still use solely face-to-face delivery for most of their L&D programmes, and a third still use this style of delivery for at least three-quarters of their training events.

Any movement towards a more independent style of learning will call for employees to "learn how to learn", to make the most of the opportunities they will be given. We must not underestimate the extent of the culture shock this will represent for some people. For many who are accustomed only to classroom-style directed learning, the move to independent learning will be a big step, and they will need support in making it. A Deloitte survey of HR developments in 2016 described the change of mindset involved as a move "away from periodic programs owned by learning professionals to self-directed solutions owned by individual employees".[35]

But "self-directed" should not come to mean "unsupported". While learners should be able to choose the subjects in which they receive development (after all, they know better than anyone the areas in

---

[33] "Learning technologies" are viewed as the whole range of digital technologies which can be used for learning, e.g. online learning, virtual classrooms, mobile apps, massive open online courses (MOOCs), and social media.

[34] Chartered Institute of Personnel and Development, *Learning and Development*, with the permission of the publisher, the Chartered Institute of Personnel and Development (www.cipd.co.uk).

[35] Deloitte, *Global Human Capital Trends 2016*.

which their knowledge or skills fall short of what is required to do the job), they must not then be set loose with no support. They must be able to turn for advice to L&D professionals whenever they need it. L&D specialists need to be guides, advisors, and enablers, rather than purely deliverers of face-to-face training.

The provision of learning opportunities needs RISK to be managed. In this context we use the acronym to stand for:

- Relevance
- Interest
- Skill focus, mindset and application required
- Knowledge needed.

The development of content that motivates through an almost self-perpetuating energy and attractiveness can help instil a seriousness into the desire for learning and improved performance.

There is clearly some way to go before we achieve this. A survey of L&D professionals in 55 countries in 2015[36] revealed that 83 per cent of the respondents wanted to increase self-directed learning in their organisations, but only 22 per cent were achieving this goal. L&D specialists themselves will also need support to make this change. They will also need to be prepared to let go to some extent, by giving employees control of their own learning.

"...business, learning, and HR leaders must embrace a new mind-set that puts learners in the driver's seat".[37]

The need to ensure that learners have the right skills to benefit from the new learning methods is underlined by the fact that a survey of over 1,600 employees worldwide in 2015 has shown that a lack of skills to manage their own learning is as powerful a barrier to the

---

[36] Towards Maturity, *Embracing Change* (2015).
[37] Deloitte, *Global Human Capital Trends 2016*.

use of digital learning as is its cost.[38] These two factors were each identified by almost two-thirds of respondents,[39] making them the greatest obstacles to the use of digital learning identified by this survey. Even though many employees will be fully conversant with MOOCs, apps, social media, and the like, this will still not apply to everyone, and no one should be disadvantaged by an absence of guidance on how to use learning technologies.

A lack of IT skills among L&D professionals themselves was identified in the same survey (by 56 per cent of respondents) as another major obstacle to implementing digital learning.[40] In 2015 the CIPD questioned L&D professionals regarding their priorities versus their assessment of the availability in their organisations of the necessary skills to deliver on these.

- 91 per cent of L&D professionals said developing digital content is a priority.
- 31 per cent had the skills in-house to do this.
- 93 per cent said the ability to use social media effectively is a priority.
- 15 per cent had the skills in-house to do this.
- 96 per cent said supporting learners online was a priority.
- 36 per cent had the skills in-house to do this.

This shortage of skills has continued. In 2016, only 30 per cent reported having the skills in-house for webinar delivery, while only a third of L&D leaders had even done an audit of the skills among their teams versus those actually required. The lesson is obvious. Some fairly basic IT training for both L&D specialists and the learners they support would be extremely valuable in breaking down many of the barriers to the use of learning technologies. For the specialists, a degree of "physician, heal thyself" would work wonders here,

---

[38] Towards Maturity, *Embracing Change* (2015)
[39] 63 per cent.
[40] Towards Maturity, *Embracing Change* (2015).

with L&D professionals hopefully showing the same enthusiasm for undergoing training themselves as we hope to engender in employees generally.

The use of learning technologies is clearly set to increase in the very near future. The 2015 CIPD survey in the UK[41] showed that, of the organisations already making some use of technologies, a quarter expected to be using them to deliver more than half of their L&D activity after another year, and 10 per cent expected to use this method for more than three-quarters of their activity in the same timescale.

Blended learning, which combines digital learning using both internal and external sources with more traditional methods such as face-to-face courses, has the virtue of catering for a range of learning preferences. It "combines the effectiveness and socialisation opportunities of the classroom with the technologically enhanced active learning possibilities of the online environment",[42] and thus offers more flexibility in regard to users' preferred learning methods.

Although widely viewed as a valuable method of training, blended learning is not yet widely used. In the CIPD's Employee Outlook survey in 2016, 81 per cent of respondents viewed blended learning as "useful" or "very useful", but only 4 per cent had received such training in the previous twelve months.[43]

The challenge, though, is who should lead the blend?

---

[41] Chartered Institute of Personnel and Development, *Learning and Development*, with the permission of the publisher, the Chartered Institute of Personnel and Development (www.cipd.co.uk).

[42] Dzubian, Hartman, and Moskal, *Blended Learning* (University of Central Florida, 2004).

[43] Chartered Institute of Personnel and Development, *Employee Outlook*, with the permission of the publisher, the Chartered Institute of Personnel and Development (www.cipd.co.uk).

As shown in the opening chapter, our view is that the responsibility of the related support function (training, learning and development, management development, talent development, leadership development, executive development, graduate development, apprentice development, and all similarly named functions) is to provide relevant opportunities to learn and develop, and to provide access through multiple channels and coordinated activity and experience. The individual and line manager should take responsibility to use those opportunities in the best way for any learning to be applied. However, in order to truly cater for the widest possible range of preferences, the most promising route is to adopt focused learning, through which L&D can provide a menu of options tailored to individual needs. Some people may need only a quick-fix option, or possibly a refresher, while others may need a longer, more detailed solution. Identifying the most appropriate combination of sources and learning methods to suit both the subject and the learner calls for a considerable level of skill and expertise, and goes right to the heart of L&D's obligation to serve the business.

The concept of neuro-agility is one that we need to take seriously if we are to meet future performance demands and undertake the learning necessary to meet them. It refers to the brain's ability to be "in flow", learning fast and effectively, committing minimal human error, and operating beyond unconscious competence. The neuroscientist Dr. Andre Vermeulen identifies the levels of "master" and "artist" in this zone. Neuro-agility is demonstrated, for example, when you see great musicians and sports people stand out with their consistently high level of skill beyond others who are all "unconsciously competent".

In 1975 Robert N Singer identified in his book Motor Learning and Human Performance that a skill is only acquired when it can be consistently reproduced under intense pressure. Forty-three years on though, we need to consider the context, and ask ourselves when do individuals need to acquire a skill, and when do they simply need to apply it in a simple way? The same is true of knowledge. In other words, when addressing the issue of the medium through which learning should be designed, developed, and delivered, it is important to take into account their frequency of need or use, and their complexity. Which of these needs could be satisfied by googling or by using internal chat rooms or video sources, which need something more, which need access to deeper content, and which need a more comprehensive suite of options?

We believe, having explored many vendor-led reports, academic papers and beyond, that the need now is for personalised learning and performance playbooks. We have seen a lot of learning referred to as "based on neuroscience", but much of it is more or less as it was beforehand, well-constructed instructional design centred on set pathways and programmes. The brain is a fantastically complex control centre, and each person has a unique interconnected mix of dominant drivers and neurological design. We are all wired differently, and thus the solutions, or rather opportunities to access learning content and application, need to be learner-led. Individuals not only need to take responsibility for their performance and learning, but also for the way they do so, and for why, when and how they make their learning work. They are also responsible for how they translate it into performance, whether in the process of acquisition or, at the other extreme, how they copy and move on.

Similarly, L&D must identify what *type* of learning is required. Depending on the topic, some things may need to be learnt and retained (learnt by heart, as it were), while with other things it may be enough to relearn (i.e. to look up the answer) when necessary. An airline pilot knows how to land his or her aircraft without any prompting (learnt by heart), but when it comes to the approach procedures for every airport the airline may fly to, no one expects the pilots to remember all the details, so they effectively relearn them on each flight by looking them up as needed.

L&D professionals are having to accept considerable change in their jobs, and some of this change can seem rather threatening, especially when it may involve directing employees to external sources of learning. But we must avoid being precious about promoting access to external sources. We must learn to let go and give learners more control. Focused learning offers the best of both worlds, with access to our own organisation's material and the very best of what's available elsewhere, and a mix of delivery methods which suit the individual and the subject. It's not an admission of failure to signpost learners to sources of learning not available internally. On the contrary, it is an illustration of our commitment to meeting employees' needs by providing them with the best material available, regardless of its source, and giving them control. This, and the combination of face-to-face and digital learning, offers some exciting possibilities for the future.

As we have already discussed, the role of the L&D professional is changing. In the CIPD survey, 46 per cent agreed with the statement "Our L&D role is shifting from that of learning delivery to consultancy."[44] Increasingly, that consultancy role will involve advising employees and their line managers to do things other than "go on a course". The role of curator will move out of museums and into the workplace, as L&D specialists research and collate resources and identify solutions to improve performance. This "curator" designation is destined to become familiar currency soon as L&D professionals stop being order-takers and become advisors and consultants, showing employees the way towards the solutions that suit them.

"Top learning organisations are moving away from training delivery as a core focus to a performance consulting model. There, the role of L&D is to diagnose problems and develop or curate the right solutions that move beyond 'the course' and equip staff for change."[45]

---

[44] Towards Maturity, *L&D: Evolving Roles, Enhancing Skills*, research report (Apr. 2015).
[45] Towards Maturity, *L&D: Evolving Roles, Enhancing Skills*, research report (Apr. 2015).

However, the speed of that change seems relatively slow. According to the CIPD,[46] only 18 per cent of L&D professionals in 2015 were planning to reduce classroom delivery, and 53 per cent agreed that the course is only one of many options for improving performance, which means that almost half are still relying only on the course. However, is this a relevant measure? We see the increase in a drive for learning and development to develop ecosystems of learning. We see the rise of in-the-moment social learning through mobile systems. All are worthy additions to the ways in which people can learn. All can have a direct impact on performance. All can be measured.

Bearing in mind the figures quoted elsewhere regarding the appetite for new methods such as digital and blended learning, this rate of change appears to leave L&D very much in the slow lane. The Towards Maturity benchmark for the three years to 2015 shows that digital learning has made tangible improvements in business performance in many organisations. The top-performing organisations in the survey reported an average improvement of 15 per cent in customer satisfaction and 12 per cent in productivity, and an 8 per cent reduction in staff turnover. Impressive figures, but they won't have any impact if we keep them to ourselves.

There is a place, though, for time in the classroom. Universities are reporting an increase in demand for classroom time to introduce, to clarify, and to explore application. Sometimes, the initial motivation or spark to learn needs a "kick-start". When you see a new book on a subject, you leave it on the shelf, deferring, if interest has not yet been aroused. This can be true of any form of "pull" or download learning. Additionally, content can result in simply being interesting.

The assumptions being portrayed as fact relating to delivery methods preferred by managers and millennials are to some extent questioned in the 2017 Good Practice report *Learning*

---

[46] Ibid.

Technologies; What Managers Really Think.[47] The report highlights the fact that face-to-face learning is perceived as more useful than digital approaches; younger managers are more open to digital approaches; managers have a high opinion of good e-learning; and mobile learning is seen by managers to offer little substance. It continues with a range of insights and confirms that all have their place. Any time in the classroom should *go beyond* interesting, go beyond being academic to be exciting and relate to application. Separately, when one of the authors was reviewing a corporate strategy, all management voted face-to-face time as important inside and outside the classroom. They reported the networking value to be highly significant and the potential for coaching time as vital. When interviewing Nigel Girling on his career in IT with Sun Microsystems, Jaguar Land Rover, VMware and BT Global Services he reflected that 'many of his most important contacts were formed during the breaks at face to face courses. Personal learning via social media, video, mobile or virtual classrooms should not kill the growth of new peer relationships and damage real communication. Both or all are needed.' In the report, managers also realised the value of the provision of learning options and of individuals being in charge of their own development, being able to access their preferred medium for specific learning needs, and able to manage their own application to performance with support.

The Good Practice report reflects that newer technologies "offer L&D lots of potential", though managers are less supportive. Accelerating learning maturity, personal blending of learning content and opportunity, with clear links and management of the learning into performance flow will be key to that potential being realised. This relates directly to the personalised learning playbooks introduced earlier.

---

[47] Owen Ferguson, Stef Scott, and Gemma Towersey, *Learning Technologies: What Managers Really Think*, research report (Good Practice, Nov. 2017).

According to a recent article by Matthew French, quoted by Bersin, providing employees the opportunity for learning and development in the workplace has become a paramount attractor in the job market, particularly given the number of millennials in the workforce and their focus on just that. Today's youth will potentially have 70-plus year careers.

French demonstrated that learning is one of the top ten HR trends for 2017. Deloitte's annual *Human Capital Trends* (HCT) report for 2016[48] illustrates the fact that "learning departments are changing from education providers to content curators and experience facilitators, developing innovative platforms that turn employee learning and development into a self-driven pursuit." This is very much in line with the approach taken by Abbey National as far back as 1997, twenty years ago. The added incentive today is, as Bersin notes, "individuals now see the link between learning and earning."

With this we believe that individuals, when convinced of the WHY' will take responsibility and open the door for strong Personalized Learning and Performance Playbooks. Working with managers and/or coaches to determine their own blend of learning that will enhance their performance, help them to grow, or simply help them to have better days in the workplace. To be more 'in flow.'

Building upon this essential consideration are a number of organisational factors. These are the 2016 Deloitte HCT findings—top 10 trends for 2017—with additional notes from our research:

1. **Organisational structure: The rise of teams**
   Hierarchical organisational models aren't just being turned upside down—they're being reconstructed from the inside out. Businesses are reinventing themselves to operate as networks of teams to keep pace with the challenges of a fluid, unpredictable world. Teams need support and awareness to

---

[48] Deloitte, *Global Human Capital Trends 2016*.

enable their team learning. Team coaching is increasing and can add significant value when focused in a facilitative role.

2. **Leadership awakened: Generations, teams, science**
    Leaders of all ages, genders, and cultures are now poised to take the reins at organisations around the world. How ready will these future business leaders be to take charge in an increasingly complex global marketplace? To what extent are the differences in people fully appreciated by leaders of all ages and cultures? The role of people expertise will be critical in managing the consequences of new challenges caused by digitalisation, social media, artificial intelligence, and beyond.

3. **Culture: Shape culture, drive strategy**
    The impact of culture on business is hard to overstate: 82 per cent of respondents to the 2016 Global Human Capital Trends survey believe that culture is a potential competitive advantage. It is also key to productivity. It can be continually influenced positively and negatively by the frameworks and policies implemented by people support. Our research indicates organisations are seeking to go beyond culture to include all facets of the working environment.

4. **Engagement: Always on and stress**
    Employee engagement and retention today means understanding an empowered workforce's desire for flexibility, creativity, and purpose. Under the evolving social contract between employer and employee, workers become "volunteers" to be re-engaged and re-recruited each day. In a separate piece of research, People in Flow identified the "always on" culture expectation as a major source of stress. Stress is unhelpful to learning and performance. The challenge of reducing stress is a vital one for the whole of people support to address. It will need to be a fully

integrated, informed, collaborative, and coordinated drive, with all involved clear on the consequences.

5. **Learning: Employees take charge**
   Corporate learning departments are changing from education providers to content curators and experience facilitators, developing innovative platforms that turn employee learning and development into a self-driven pursuit. The drive to provide opportunities to learn and perform will require significant mindset shifts by all involved. The concept previously noted of Personalized Learning and Performance Playbooks relates directly to this trend.

6. **Design thinking: Crafting the employee experience**
   Design thinking takes aim at the heart of unnecessary workplace complexity by putting the employee experience first—helping to improve productivity by designing solutions that are at once compelling, enjoyable, and simple. These new processes through a simpler approach also raise people challenges. Are managers managing the process or the people, or both?

7. **People Support: Growing momentum toward a new mandate**
   Good news: The 2016 Global Human Capital Trends survey shows an improvement in the people support organisation's skills, business alignment, and ability to innovate. But as companies change the way they are organised, they must embrace the changing role of people support as well. The commercial mindset is growing, and there are some great examples of initiatives driven by people support that directly impact the bottom line and future planning. Barratt Developments plc in the UK, are one such example with their Armed Forces Transition Programme. It not only is making a direct impact upon the business but also can transform the industry. The well-considered, aligned, integrated,

proactively managed, continually improved, efficient, and effective programme has already made a sustained impact on the sites managed by Barratt Homes.

8. **People analytics: Gaining speed**
   The use of analytics in people support is growing, with organisations aggressively building people-analytics teams, buying analytics offerings, and developing analytics solutions. People support now has the chance to demonstrate ROI or impact on its analytics efforts, helping to make the case for further focused investment. It can support the shift in value perception and lead continual improvement within your unique organisation.

9. **Digital: People support revolution, not evolution**
   A new world for people support technology and design teams is on the horizon. Mobile and other technologies could allow people support leaders to revolutionise the employee experience through new digital platforms, apps, and ways of delivering people support services. This must be considered in context. The helpfulness, range, and depth of these platforms need all contribute, yet there is real energy potential when done well.

10. **The gig economy: Distraction or disruption?**
    How can a business manage talent effectively when many, or even most, of its people, are not actually its employees? Networks of people who work without any formal employment agreement—as well as the growing use of machines as talent—are reshaping the talent management equation.

We will look further at some of these trends within the book, identifying which are need-driven versus which are vendor-led, which matter, and which should be taken and embraced in our stride as professionals.

The Bersin report highlights an example of a high-impact learning culture. Our view is, to quote a sporting analogy, "If you focus on the result, you are unlikely to achieve it." The need is to focus on the act, not the consequence. In this context, the need is to focus on performance and the learning needed that will be accessed.

High-Impact Learning Culture®

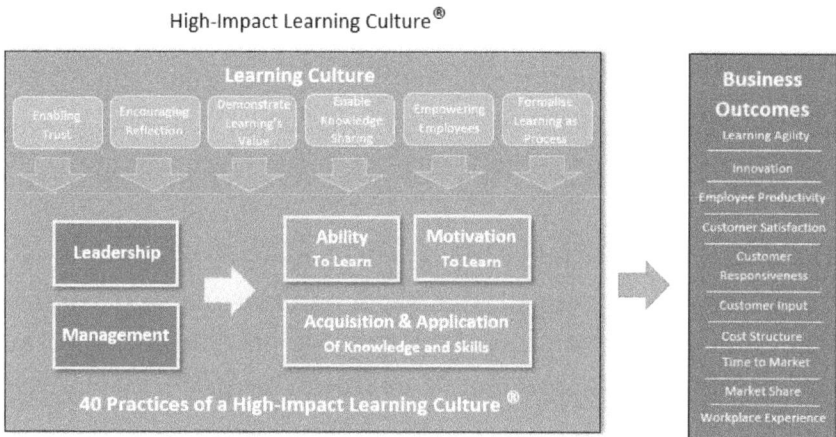

Copyright Bersin and Associates by Deloitte. Used with permission.

Bersin's high-impact learning culture model, above, shows seven elements of a robust learning culture. All are challenges for many organisations. We would tip the model. The business outcomes need to drive the components of a learning culture, and the taking of responsibility for performance and development for continued optimal performance rests with every individual. Clarity on the business outcomes is key. This is why a detailed and considered review of learning supply is important. It is performance-required learning that will drive methodology for individuals. The clamour for digital *only* to replace classroom learning or e-learning is driven by technology development. Digital learning is good, but not by itself. We must not fall for the same single-thought rationale for e-learning of the late 1990s and early 2000s. There is no "snake oil"; there are considered strategies for supply, access, and application.

We agree with the essence of the Bersin model but believe stepping stones are vital.

Opportunity	Trust & Commitment	Environment
Engagement		Responsibility
Business Outcomes linked to Strategy, purpose & Intent		

The strategies contained within the Bersin model largely fit inside this framework, along with the leader and management skill sets that enable the letting go of control, the informed, integrated, collaborative, and coordinated approach to performance that encourages learning.

The one problem we have is that while it is fine to demonstrate the value of learning, it is the focus on impact from learning that is the key. The learning simply needs to be worth the effort, time, and investment.

There are several solution-focused models and frameworks in existence; an awareness of these can aid you in determining the best way to provide opportunity in your organisation and encourage people to take opportunity through whichever way they are learning—informally, in role, or through the access to support provided within systems, either socially or within facilitated opportunity. Frameworks such as 70:20:10[49] can help to provide a context and rationale. Vendors can provide compelling evidence to position a new product or strategy. Ultimately, you must manage this for your organisation.

We have already discussed the use of data and analysis techniques to illustrate the performance and business alignment of people

---

[49] Arets and Jennings, *702010 Towards 100% performance* (2016)

support in general, but the same importance attaches to the use of data by L&D professionals in particular. A survey by *Chief Learning Officer* magazine[50] showed that two-thirds of chief learning officers[51] reported that their organisations had at least some capacity for using technology to collect and analyse data from people support systems. Other results of this survey were revealing:

- L&D reports to the board on return on investment in learning   19.2 per cent
- L&D reports to the board on employee engagement   45.8 per cent
- Board never requests learning data or analytics   34.3 per cent
- Business analysts never request learning data   48.8 per cent

There is possibly a degree of chicken-and-egg in this situation. To what extent are boards, for example, not requesting the data because they have never seen them in the past and simply don't know what is available? And business analysts are usually data junkies—they can't get enough of the stuff—so if they know something is available, they will normally snap it up. Perhaps the apparent lack of interest from these groups is because they have just not been offered the data in the past. Could we be guilty either of being reluctant to bang the L&D drum or of lacking the analytical skills to make use of the data available?

The authors are not great fans of office politics, but we have seen first-hand in several organisations just how highly business analysts are regarded and how much influence they have with the board. They also, of course, have a high level of skills in data analysis. But they can't report on what they don't even see, so if you feel that your

---

[50] Human Capital Media, "2016 Survey of Measurement and Metrics", *Chief Learning Officer* (2016), covering 227 L&D professionals.
[51] 65.5 per cent.

L&D function is being overlooked and you want its performance data to be noticed, try feeding in data via the business analysts. What they have to say tends to get the board's attention, so taking this route offers a good chance of showing the decision-makers just how L&D is contributing to the business. It's a bit like product placement in television shows. Getting L&D data into presentations by the business analysts will get our activities noticed by the people who make the big decisions in the organisation.

Of all the areas of people support, L&D is probably the one most vulnerable to being outsourced. As we all know, external consultants are frequently brought in to deliver specific activities, and this seems likely to continue. The CIPD's 2015 survey of L&D[52] showed more or less equal numbers of respondents expecting their organisations to increase the use of external consultants over the following two years, compared with those who expected this to decline.[53] According to Bersin by Deloitte,[54] external provision has declined dramatically, from 41 per cent in 2009 to 14 per cent in 2015, but with training budgets increasing post-recession, bringing in external providers may sometimes still be seen as a quick-fix solution.

L&D professionals therefore have the greatest incentive among all people support specialists to prove their value to the organisation by showing how their activities impact upon the aims of the business. However, they all too frequently fail to do themselves justice in this respect. As we have already seen, L&D departments, even where they gather data on return on investment, employee engagement, or the overall impact of their work on the business, often fail to report on these topics to the board.

---

[52] Chartered Institute of Personnel and Development, *Learning and Development*, with the permission of the publisher, the Chartered Institute of Personnel and Development (www.cipd.co.uk).

[53] 26 per cent expected an increase; 25 per cent expected a decline.

[54] Karen O'Leonard, *The UK Learning Factbook 2013: Benchmarks, Trends, and Analysis of the UK Training Market* (Bersin by Deloitte, 2013).

We have already discussed the need for people support generally to align with the business, and this is equally important for L&D in particular. It is essential to be able to show clearly how L&D affects individual and business performance. However, the L&D function has been slow to develop the necessary skills. In 2013 the Learning and Performance Institute surveyed almost a thousand L&D professionals, and concluded: "The results suggest that the profession lacks the broader, business-based skills it will need to contribute as part of the organisation of the future."[55]

As the 2015 CIPD research report on L&D says: "We need to ensure that there is a clear line of sight between L&D activity and organisational performance."[56] This can only be achieved if L&D professionals have a good knowledge of business aims and processes, and the skills to enable them to interpret their own data and present the results to managers.

L&D Conclusions

As a group, L&D professionals are perhaps guilty of promoting the benefits of learning to other people and then sometimes failing to follow their own advice when it comes to developing their own skills. As the CIPD's 2015 survey of L&D points out, "So often, we deprioritise our own development, as we spend our time focusing on others, rather than ourselves."[57] This is especially true in two areas, digital skills and analytics. Despite emerging as current priorities in all the research and surveys consulted in the writing of this book, these seem to remain areas of weakness within the people support profession in general. If anything, this trend seems to be even more apparent among L&D professionals. However, when digital learning of all kinds is becoming increasingly important

---

[55] The Learning and Performance Institute Limited, *The LPI Capability Map, Six-Month Report* (June 2013).
[56] Towards Maturity, *L&D: Evolving Roles*.
[57] Ibid.

for employees, and the analysis of data to support decision-making is a priority for CEOs, acquiring skills in these areas will allow people support professionals, whether generalists or L&D specialists, to show their value to the business.

"In order to maximise resources and evolve roles to best meet business needs, L&D must address key skill gaps. These primarily include business and commercial understanding, facilitation of social learning and technological capability, alongside skills that enable robust diagnosis and the development or curation of the right solutions."[58]

The authors have experience of L&D in both the public and private sectors, and want the profession to prosper and to be seen as the valuable asset it genuinely is. We believe that the best way to ensure that this happens is for L&D professionals not just to *embrace* change in learning practice but also to *lead* it, to *shape* the future rather than merely adapt to developments. Doing this will involve taking on unfamiliar roles and learning new, perhaps unexpected, skills. Some of this will be difficult, possibly even scary, but don't we constantly urge other people to put their fears behind them and learn by undertaking new experiences?

Improving digital skills is an absolute necessity; we make no apology for repeating this. We don't need to become programmers or web designers, but we do need to be able to develop digital content which will engage learners and match their learning preferences. We also need to be able to use the technology for which the content is designed. Technology is moving quickly; the challenge is to ensure that it will really help your people to learn and perform. Where will mixed reality take us? It is a step on from virtual reality, and at this moment whether to use video, whether to work video and social networking together, whether to use build or flow techniques with content, whether to let go or control, are all challenges. Yet they offer real opportunity for expertise to add value.

---

[58] Ibid.

The skills to manipulate, analyse, and present data are equally important, and are key to ensuring that L&D receives due credit for its contribution to the business.

We also need to be prepared to move into new areas. The "curator" role will involve L&D professionals creating not just blended but also *focused* learning, by identifying a wide range of sources, content, methods, and technologies to suit both the individual learner and the subject. Use RISK to enable content that attracts.

Attracting and retaining talent (particularly by providing innovative, challenging learning opportunities), promoting employee engagement, and enabling better decision-making at board level can only serve to take people support (and especially L&D) from "valued" to "valuable". More on this later.

The need for the taking of responsibility by the learner is critical. The support and guidance roles of coaches and line managers are also important in ensuring the flow from learning into performance. Let it happen and encourage it—without asking for judgement at this stage. We have referenced the link with performance; let us now explore that further, and the challenges this brings to bear.

Go beyond performance

Performance management = performance enablement

A Handbook of Personnel Management Practice[59] defines performance management as being "about getting better results from the organisation, teams and individuals by understanding and managing performance within an agreed framework of planned goals, standards and competence requirements".

---

[59] M. Armstrong, *A Handbook of Personnel Management Practice* (Kogan Page, 1995).

There has been a problem with an inconsistent appreciation of the term "performance management". For some it is interpreted as appraisals; for others, a process of annual or half yearly/quarterly formal reviews; for others, a laborious and unnecessary completion of HR online boxes; and still others, an unfair and variable way of ratings and maybe getting bonuses. The interpretations go on. They are all potential components or even consequences of a process-driven approach.

Often, managers and individuals perceive performance management as a burden. But what exactly is the burden? What are the responsibilities that pertain to performance? What is the purpose of your role, and how does it relate to company intent? What responsibilities do you each have to meet the basic salary being paid? Are you earning it, and are you achieving your expected performance and intent?

As members of the people support profession, we invest billions in reviewing structures and processes, and spend a significant amount of time and money on leadership, management, and talent training programmes. We attempt to lift levels of knowledge through accredited academic programmes for those we believe to be key employees. Is what we have been investing in to make the difference actually achieving our intent? Are we seeking to *really* make a difference, or are we in an organisation where underperformance against potential is acceptable. And what is the importance of effective management and the embodiment of values?

Many business leaders find performance management attractive in theory and yet risky in practice. Some feel that performance management can be counterproductive. Among the common complaints are that it becomes irrelevant quickly as the business changes faster than the system; that it is ineffective because managers wait too long to provide feedback; that performance reviews don't help employees develop; and that ranking and rating reduces engagement and demotivates employees. Other drivers for change have been frustration of all involved with overburdening technology systems, and the illusion of unfairness (the CIPD found that 30 per cent of UK employees felt their employer's appraisal process was unfair[60]).

These may all be valid, yet it is in the implementation rather than the philosophy that the problems arise. The issues are within the system and a fundamental interpretation of responsibility.

For optimal performance to be achieved at individual, team, department, and organisation level, every individual, every day, must take responsibility for their own performance, for their own development, and for the performance and development of those they work alongside. It is in this order that responsibility leads to results. When achieving optimal performance as a leader or manager, your own performance includes how well you enable the contribution of all. One more factor for the change in approach quoted is "management disillusionment". Towers Watson found that almost half of the companies they surveyed were not seeing value in performance management and appraisals, despite it being their responsibility to ensure value is achieved.[61]

Perhaps, then, it is performance enablement that we are seeking to achieve, and the systems intended to support it are the *management* of performance enablement.

In the last three years since 2014 we have seen many high-profile organisations lead a drift towards the reviewing of performance management, along with headlines such as "The end of performance management" and "Performance management isn't working", and

---

[60] Claire Churchard, "Appraisals deemed unfair by one-third of employees, finds CIPD', People Management, May 2014

[61] Willis Towers Watson, *How to Build a Compelling Employee Value Proposition* (Jan. 2014).

similar bold statements. Companies such as Deloitte, Accenture, and Microsoft; local government bodies; and others have declared their intent to change. What has followed is a degree of copying.

What have they changed? The removal of ratings, the removal of appraisals, the increase of basic pay, and a reduction in objective-related bonuses—or at least a rebalancing. These things may help in some organisations, but in others the culture still needs them. Any system support and IT support must add to the ease of managing action such as enabling the increase in real-time coaching and feedback, and the reduction of time spent with the technology in return for more time with the people. In some organisations, it may be the technology, rather than the concept, that requires review. In all, the approach has to enable the organisation's purpose and intent, and time has to be spent ensuring the clear alignment.

What is required of performance management is that it *enable*. It must support motivation, release potential, be able to adapt with the business, and be designed with and for the business. Its intentions need to be clear, and all involved must be committed to their responsibilities in achievement.

The legacy of poor process, practice, and systems has given performance management a bad name. However, good design of the overall system, one that fits your own unique company needs, culture, values, and intent, and a strong implementation fully endorsed and committed to by all, will always add value to interactions and performance results. It can be daunting and requires careful planning, perhaps something a lot of managers are reluctant to do.

Performance enablement should be the art that moves with the science of performance management rather than monitoring. It should generate positive energy rather than be the cause of cyclical detachment and disengagement. Most of all, it must be for your company and owned by all.

The truth is that many organisations do not do it well, even after a good start. This is a shame, given that everyone at work on day one was perceived as talent, bringing skills to the organisation, motivated and wanting to do well, wanting to make a valuable contribution. Maintaining this "day one energy" is an underpinning challenge and requirement.

To achieve this, the challenge is to adapt the way managers and employees think about and use performance management, not purely for their own gains. When achieved, it is then possible to simplify and build on success by extending the benefits of excellence in performance management into other areas that depend on it, for example talent and succession.

What of objectives? Research has shown that when appropriate, when relevant, when linked to intended results and purpose, when contribution to wider success is clear, when flexible, and when committed to, objectives provide a framework that motivates. The framework also enables a freedom appropriate to situational management that enhances that motivation.

One of the authors was privileged to learn hugely from an experience of spending a day with the Royal Shakespeare Company in Stratford-upon-Avon. Yes, he had paid for the tickets; yes, he was entertained; yes, he was treated to a wonderful production and fabulous acting. These were all hoped for. There was, however, an unexpected bonus: he learnt.

He had paid a small amount extra to attend a morning session called Production Unwrapped. The production was *The Tempest*; the session was delivered by Aileen Gonsalves (the assistant director) and two of the cast, Sarah Kameela Impey and Oliver Towse, and hosted by one of the management team. Aileen and the cast members treated those attending to an insight into how the production was built from first rehearsal upwards. The most compelling and brilliant element was their use of "instant objectives".

Aileen explained that her use of objectives was to create a response, a string of thought and action, a reaction. It is for the immediate situation and scene. Try your response. She would simply check progress by asking, "Is it working?" The actor then assessed his or her situation and, if necessary, adjusted, changed tactics, or built on what was working.

For offices, for sales or project teams, for activities of the now in the achievement of bigger goals and within operating frameworks, this use of instant objectives—review and adjust—provides an energy and rhythm that is compelling. It empowers, it involves, it engages.

Why have appraisals that demotivate?

There is a lot of energy behind the removal of performance management reviews. Logically, this is a solid move if they are currently demotivating, overly false, and badly linked to reward.

However, in organisations where the intended results are supported by them and they are done well, why change? What are they for, to manage and control performance or to encourage greater commitment and contribution? Depending on the role and industry, it could be either. Leaders and managers should be asking whether the objectives, and the way they use them, are creating the working environment that their organisation needs. Are any subcultures acceptable, and do they remain aligned to wrap-around values? Are teams being allowed to create the workflows that optimise their skill sets and productivity? Do these enhance customer experience?

What, then, are the demands of the managers, beyond their responsibility to enable the intended results with the people they work with? If administration and bureaucracy outweigh the value, if they take away the ability to walk the floor and enable on a regular basis, then people support is in the way. If it supports, then people support is contributing value. This will depend on each unique organisation's situation.

Finally, we arrive at the questions that underpin all the issues behind the achievement of optimal performance at all levels. Are managers judges or enablers? Are they controllers or releasers? Are managers hindering their employees' learning and development and stifling performance? Do they have the skill sets that make the approach work for all? Are they able to operate in an integrated, informed, coordinated, and collaborative way across the organisation and ensure consistency in implementation and commitment?

For so many centuries we have defaulted to system and process change to make a difference, ignoring the power of the fully released energy of all those we employ to add value and to bring their strengths to the products and services we offer to others. An island-based telecommunications company recently conducted some research with a leading university. The executive and senior managers were concerned that after a lot of investment in people-related support and significant investment in change, there were still some significant shortcomings against hoped- for levels of performance. The assumption was that the individual staff were still resisting change and that management were not strong enough to influence them.

The findings showed that the management and staff were all totally behind the changes, were equipped and willing. It was the controls introduced by the executive to ensure success that were getting in the way. HR/people support were spending so much time complying that they had little energy left to add value and fully commit. The systems and processes that enabled the executive to measure, *manage*, and discuss were negatively impacting the achievement of intent.

Should people support and learning focus on compliance or add value or both? In some groups, the desire for management to control everything may override a need to let expertise play and to work with expertise. Are those within people support perceived by management as experts whose contributions could add value?

We recently asked an organisation, "Do you enable a natural flow from learning to performance?" There was just one thing to check: What was asked at the end of training? This is a crucial point in the transfer of learning to performance. So, do you ask a full set of "happy sheet" questions that ask the delegate to assess his or her satisfaction with a whole range of things? Once you ask such questions, you introduce a new role—not of learner or performer but of judge! Once you ask employees to judge, their responsibility to take their learning into performance is blocked. We have found that the "What has been learnt?", "What is planned as a result?", and "What value do you perceive being added as a result?" types of questions can be answered from a variety of other sources, and that a serious application of learning to performance activity at this point and beyond can really add to the impact of your investment in learning.

One thing to reflect upon: common practice does not mean best practice. What works for one culture and organisation may well not be appropriate in another. People leaders, individual contributors, and employees alike must acquire both the skills and attitudes necessary for such an approach to become routine. Skills such as the ability to hold difficult discussions, motivational discussions, and supportive discussions, to enable environments, and to commit to performance are all vital. Reviews of what is needed in your organisation should not be just tinkering with the process, but rather igniting a truly revolutionary new methodology, mindset, and *performance.* Whether this deserves the label of ideal remains to be seen.

In embracing performance management *and* enablement, our findings certainly throw light upon the debates surrounding management, leadership, talent development, and performance management. Within people support we need to be clear that we are enabling the natural flow of people and performance.

Onwards to the transfer and the role of traditional performance reviews. The link with development opportunities or areas for improvement is assumed but often not made. Has your review ever included a discussion about your growth? What new skills and knowledge have you acquired? How are you putting them to use? What value do you contribute? Is the growth arc sufficient, timely, and appropriate? Do you need to ramp up acquisition of new skills or better utilise the ones you already possess? Taking responsibility as an individual, every employee should be monitoring their growth as a step on the path to improving contribution. Managers and leaders should be gauging employee growth on an individual and collective basis to better manage talent and frame acquisition and development plans.

To bring it alive, performance management should not be relegated to a calendar-determined process or event-driven activity. The ideal performance management cycle is simply that—an ongoing interactive dialogue which encompasses contributions, perseverance, and growth.

The timing can depend on the situation, just as with the Royal Shakespeare Company example earlier. Supervisors, team leaders, and managers will need to shift from "performance reviews" thinking to an approach that is iterative and timely, one that really manages and enables optimal performance. Such an approach mandates reliance on trust building, constructive confrontation, and crucial conversations.

People leaders, individual contributors, and employees alike must acquire both the skills and the attitudes necessary for such an approach to become routine. This is not just tinkering with the process, but rather igniting a truly revolutionary methodology.

We will explore the role of reward strategy and payroll structure reviews later. Suffice to say that there needs to be a clear alignment with what you want to achieve and who you want to be as an organisation. There needs to be an alignment to the way in which optimal performance is encouraged, but this does not necessarily link to a formal process. Be clear on what are you trying to achieve. What is the intended impact, and what are the drivers that you need to unleash?

The challenges with talent and succession management

"Talent management is the process by which an organisation identifies, manages and develops its people now and for the future."[62]

To develop what? Expected and optimal performance now and in the future.

A global survey of over three hundred CEOs, chief financial officers, and HR (people support) directors of large companies in 2012[63] found that 43 per cent of respondents felt that a failure to manage talent is to blame for poor company performance, and 40 per cent said it reduced their firm's ability to innovate.

---

[62] James A. Cannon and Rita McGee, *Talent Management and Succession Planning* (2nd edn, London: Chartered Institute of Personnel and Development, 2010)
[63] *Talent Pipeline Draining Growth*, Economist Intelligence Unit, on behalf of the Chartered Institute of Management Accountants (CIMA) and the American Institute of Certified Public Accountants (AICPA), *Talent Pipeline Draining Growth* (2012).

In the CIPD's 2015 Resourcing and Talent Planning survey, half of the CEOs surveyed had talent management as a key priority.[64] In the section on data analysis, we comment on the fairly obvious importance of providing your CEO with what he or she wants and needs. If talent management is one of your CEO's priorities, then what better way to show him or her how valuable the people support function is than to address that priority?

Let's look at some other key points from the CIPD survey:[65]

- Over three-quarters of CEOs had experienced recruitment difficulties in the previous year (i.e. 2014).
- Skill shortages were escalating.
- There was little change in the practices employed to reduce recruitment difficulties.
- Only 15 per cent of respondents reported that their organisation calculates the cost of labour turnover.

Clearly, addressing any of these areas will mean you are directly tackling one of the CEO's priorities, and there can be few better ways of showing that people support is aligning its activity with the needs of the business. Conversely, *failing* to address these matters is a pretty sure way of perpetuating the idea of people support as being on the periphery of things, not really contributing to the organisation's performance.

One of the authors once worked in a team in which turnover among the most junior staff was extremely high. However, instead of addressing the main problem (low pay), the organisation expended a huge amount of management and people support time (and money) on simply recruiting new people and training

---

[64] Chartered Institute of Personnel and Development, *Resourcing and Talent Planning* (2015), with the permission of the publisher, the Chartered Institute of Personnel and Development, (www.cipd.co.uk).
[65] Ibid.

them to do the job, only to see many of them leave after a short time. No one stopped to calculate the cost of paying the existing employees a bit more, versus continuing with this merry-go-round of recruit–train–replace.

The CIPD survey results above show that the overwhelming majority of people support departments similarly fail to make such calculations. If it's not rocket science (and it's not, let's be honest), then why are so many people support teams not doing this? And if it's a priority for the CEO, then why isn't it a people support priority as well? Where it is done, it is often analysed in isolation rather than with the onboarding, training, policy, and related people support and development teams with whom a wider picture could be formed.

In 2012 the PricewaterhouseCoopers survey of CEOs found that "skills shortages are seen as a top threat to business expansion." This survey also identified the effect in the previous year of "talent constraints" on the CEOs surveyed:

- 31 per cent were unable to innovate effectively;
- 29 per cent were unable to pursue a market opportunity;
- 24 per cent cancelled or delayed a strategic objective.

Clearly, anything people support can do to alleviate this problem will have a significant, measurable impact upon the organisation's performance. And there are very few things more effective in getting you noticed than the act of making someone else's life a bit easier. And if that person happens to be the CEO, then the effect is even greater.

We keep emphasising the importance of aligning people support activities with the objectives of the business ("start with the business"), but with good reason, because it brings the people support function the recognition it deserves, and argues strongly for it to be given a say in the organisation's strategic decision-making.

Tackling a long-established and damaging issue such as problems with the recruitment and deployment of the organisation's talent would clearly raise people support's standing in the organisation and be of obvious benefit to the business as a whole.

Data analysis offers a means of tackling some of the problems raised by the need to manage talent more effectively. The use of workforce data, which we have already discussed, is one example of the way in which people support can have this impact. The car manufacturer BMW[66] used the analysis of workforce data to identify where the largest gaps would occur among its employees in the coming decade because of a large number of long-serving staff leaving the company on retirement. As a report by Deloitte points out, financial services firms are using analysis to predict potential problems with compliance and ethics, adding, "A tool that accurately forecasts which employees are most at risk of committing ethical transgressions offers a critical insight."[67]

So, we have a situation where just about everyone involved can see there is a problem, a skills, mindset, knowledge or "applied capability" gap, but progress towards closing such gaps is slow, and over 80 per cent of HR professionals assess their own analytical ability as low.[68] The management of talent must therefore embrace the growth among people support professionals of analytical skills as an addition to the already wide range of competencies required of this group. It may be that the skills for analysis can be imported into people support by redeploying people already inside your organisation. Or perhaps it will involve importing the expertise when needed, agreeing with other departments to "borrow" the relevant people when necessary.

---

[66] KPMG and the Economist Intelligence Unit, *Rethinking Human Resources in a Changing World* (2012).

[67] Deloitte, *Global Human Capital Trends 2015: Leading in the new world of work*, (Deloitte University Press, 2015).

[68] Ibid.

The serious shortage of talent as a barrier to recruitment, identified by all the research consulted in the writing of this book, argues strongly for making the most of the talent which already exists in an organisation. A 2012 report on talent management[69] commented: "In this economic climate, organisations are more likely to develop existing employees than recruit new talent." This applies to all areas of work, including analytical skills, which, as we have seen, are only just beginning to emerge as relevant to people support work. In the same report, three-quarters of business leaders and two-thirds of people support leaders said that their organisations were more likely to develop existing talent than recruit new talent.[70]

We often tend to pigeonhole people, which blinkers our perception of their potential for redeployment, but skilful talent management enables people to break free from the limitations of "silo thinking" and enter new areas of work. The fact that someone has until now devoted their time to analysing data relating to production rates or quality control matters, for example, doesn't mean they can't work equally well with people support data. Talent-spotting people in one department whose skills could be used to greater effect in another part of the organisation is an important capability, and one which is often lacking.

"We have observed that organisations are often extremely poor at promoting high-potential candidates across divisions, so it's important to make a special effort to break through silos to identify promising inside-outsiders working in other units."[71]

---

[69] Amanda Potter and Sarah Linton, *The Future of Talent Management* (Zircon Management Consulting, May 2012).
[70] Amanda Potter and Sarah Linton, *The Future of Talent Management* (Zircon Management Consulting, May 2012).
[71] Nohria Groysberg and Fernandez-Araoz, "The Definitive Guide to Recruiting in Good Times and Bad", *Harvard Business Review* (May 2009).

This becomes a bit of a circular argument in a way, because the ability to develop existing talent into new areas of work calls for good data on the organisation's employees, as well as the skills to interpret the data. Accurate, up-to-date information on employees' skills, experience, and aptitudes allows their potential to be identified, while analytical skills allow the organisation to forecast its future needs.

External recruitment always carries with it the risk of failure, and even when successful it is expensive and time-consuming, so internal recruitment is attractive from the point of view of economy. In addition, recruiting and developing talent internally sends the message to employees that the organisation places a high value on its people, and recognises their skills and quality of performance. This approach has been shown to have a positive impact on retention, performance, and the resilience of the whole organisation, not just those involved in the talent-development process.

While we are on the subject of spotting potentially "hidden" internal talent, and with shameless self-interest as the authors both reach the age of sixty, let's put in a well-deserved plug for the (inevitably older) employees who have had previous careers. They have often acquired skills which can be of considerable value in an organisation but which have, until now, been overlooked because they are not of immediate relevance to their current role. Accurate information on their previous employment can reap dividends if it means discovering that the organisation already has skills which are rare in the external marketplace. These older employees were talent on day one!

As we have already emphasised, talent management and succession planning, like all people support activities, must serve the requirements of the organisation. Recruiting people with the required skills, or developing those skills in existing employees, ensures that these processes are aligned with the organisation's aims and objectives. Cannon and McGee refer rather coyly to one of the elements of talent management as "establishing suitable approaches to deal with those who no longer fit organisation requirements", [72] and handling redundancy is indeed one of the most challenging tasks of the many which fall to people support professionals. Those of us who have experienced redundancy know that it can be a hugely demoralising episode in anyone's life, and when the *post*, as well as the individual, is deemed to no longer fit organisation requirements, it is even more difficult to face, leading the individual to question why he or she has been coming to work all these years, if the organisation now considers it can do without the work of that post. Having to deliver the news of redundancy to others is both a sobering and an instructive experience.

An organisation's reputation is at stake when dealing with staff redundancy. If times are hard enough to require redundancies, then it is just the moment when an organisation does not need the added burden of bad publicity.

Managing the departure of employees from an organisation, whether that departure is enforced or voluntary, is a fundamental element of talent management, and it calls for the organisation to possess mature, efficient methods of identifying candidates for redundancy (including good data from people support). It equally calls for honesty and transparency in the organisation's decision-making and actions.

But one fundamental requirement for improving talent management is simply to ensure that managers engage with their organisation's strategy for doing so. In 2012 a survey of 150 HR, talent, and business leaders revealed that a third of them simply did not know or understand their organisation's talent management strategy.[73]

---

[72] Cannon and McGee, *Talent Management and Succession Planning* (2011), with the permission of the publisher, the Chartered Institute of Personnel and Development (www.cipd.co.uk).

[73] 32 per cent (Potter and Linton, *The Future of Talent Management*).

It is up to people support to educate employees throughout the organisation on the importance of talent management.

Succession management

Taking this analysis one step further in relation to talent, it is now possible to create the right match between strategic goals, required core competencies, and the desired and existing human resources asset. This then opens the door to directly link performance management and enablement with talent management and development through to succession management.

What does this need to achieve within your organisation? It needs to go beyond the flip chart and inconvenient meetings to reflective and well-considered thought enhanced by strong data feeds. The steps involved include defining the organisation's core competencies and core positions; mapping key employees and evaluating potential at the organisational level and within each organisational unit; identifying the strength of the managerial backbone; and generating the ability to create managerial reserves for core positions. In doing so, you are identifying ongoing management of risks, evaluating whether core position holders are key to leave the organisation, evaluating the readiness of potential replacements, and evaluating what impact the departure of core employees could have on the organisation.

When utilising a system such as the People in Flow Learning Beyond Data (LBD) system developed with OD Consulting, an auto-feed enables deep and rich conversation focused on action rather than the analysis.

People support, in accelerating the process of succession, frees up time to ensure objective succession is achieved. The creating of value through time savings and deeper insight is a major step in moving from valued to valuable.

Conclusions

Employees' access to people support must be quick and easy, and offer ease of access comparable to that enjoyed by customers who contact the organisation. Providing a user-friendly service and accurate information will help to raise both the profile and the reputation of people support within the organisation.

While the availability and accuracy of the service provided by people support will raise the function's standing in the eyes of employees at all levels, a capacity to produce data which will enable the forecasting of requirements will win respect at board level. Addressing the shortage of analytical skills within people support departments is a priority in both private-and public-sector organisations, one which will certainly repay the investment of time and effort needed to tackle it. Providing data which enable evidence-based decision-making allows people support to show it can align itself directly with the priorities of the business, and defends it against accusations of having an "ivory tower" mentality.

In an environment in which a shortage of people with the right skills is a problem affecting organisations of all kinds, talent management is a crucial function for people support. When recruiting new employees with the appropriate skills is difficult, making best use of the skills of existing ones is especially important. Once again, accurate data and its analysis will help identify skills already held in the organisation, across all departments and functions. Showing appreciation for existing employees in this way also sends a very positive message about the organisation's attitude towards its people.

The use of social media offers a source of information which individuals themselves enter and keep up to date. It is thus a source of views and attitudes unlikely to be recorded anywhere else, relating to both existing and prospective employees. Being able to tap into data of this kind is an invaluable opportunity, but one which is still exploited by only a small proportion of organisations.

We have laid heavy emphasis on the need within the people support function for analytical skills and the ability to manage talent effectively. Developing these skills will be a challenge, but it must be seized as an opportunity which will pay dividends in terms of raising the standing of people support within the organisation.

Management and leadership impact

The manager balance sheet challenge

Why is this an issue?

The extent to which processes can be continually improved to meet new challenges is reducing with each change. In contrast, the value and contribution of people is increasingly becoming the most viable change and improvement lever. The capability of managers and leaders to create the best working environments for all is central to this, yet experience is variable. Still we see line managers as a significant reason for leaving.

A survey by B2B marketplace identified that 42 per cent of employees have left a job because of a bad boss. In its survey of 1,374 employees two years ago, the CIPD found that almost a third (30 per cent) of employees feel their current boss is a bad manager. At that time, recruitment was ranked as the worst industry for terrible managers, with all respondents from that profession reporting that they had left a job because of a poor relationship with a manager. Other sectors which scored poorly in the survey include travel and tourism (77 per cent of respondents had left a job because of a poor manager), marketing and PR (63 per cent), and accounting (61 per cent). Other industries featuring in the top ten for worst bosses were events, entertainment, fashion, agriculture and food, architecture, and security. In the public sector, there are daily examples of stress-related illness and absence, regularly reported because of poor people-management practice.

One of the more significant manager impacts, in addition to those employees leaving, is the cost of those off with stress caused by managers.

The Health and Safety Executive has identified six factors that can lead to work-related stress if they are not managed properly, all of which are in the gift of management.

1. **Demands**
   Employees indicate that they are not able to cope with the demands of their jobs especially when micromanaged, or with constantly changing priorities.

2. **Control**
   Employees indicate that they are not able to have a say in the way they do their work.

3. **Support**
   Employees indicate that they don't receive adequate information and support from their colleagues and superiors, information, help, and consideration not being forthcoming.

4. **Relationships**
   Employees indicate that they are subjected to unacceptable behaviours, for example bullying, at work.

5. **Role**
   Employees indicate that they are confused by their role and responsibilities and don't understand the link to the overall organisation intent, purpose, and/or objectives.

6. **Change**
   Employees indicate that the organisation doesn't engage them when undergoing an organisational change.

With this in mind, to what extent do you assess the behavioural impact, actions, and net results achieved by managers when reviewing employee performance? What would help to bring this to the fore? Data and the awareness of underlying factors that influence in the form of a balance sheet would help.

What is the "in flow" balance sheet?

Every day the performance of individuals and teams is assessed against results. Are these results always what they seem to be? Is there a counterbalance to the high-level results?

Consider the balance sheet.

Positive Impact	Negative Impact
Results	Underperformance level
Moments of brilliance	Moments of interference
Extent of positive interaction with team	Attrition through negative manager actions and behaviour
Innovative contribution	Grievances
Impact of individuals and team—delegated impact	Time spent in unnecessary meetings/unproductive people issues
Analysis quality	Absence through stress

Responsibility taken for development	Lack of coaching and development support
Timing perfection	Negative management impact on productivity
Momentum management	Lack of involvement and enablement of expert contribution
Refocus interventions	Ego and political focus ahead of team value
Enabled action	Acceptance of negative-impact behaviour, e.g. bullying
Engagement levels within team	Lack of situational adaptation

What does each measure mean? People in Flow Ltd have refined and defined each measure to ensure simplicity and an easy way to survey and generate related data. In a complex working environment, it is essential that support processes, frameworks, and performance initiatives be simple to apply and that, once applied, they make a difference.

Who is involved?

Anyone in a supervisory, management, or leadership role takes responsibility for performance. They take responsibility for their own performance, their own development, and the performance and development of others they work with and lead/manage. With responsibility comes the need to create, ensure, encourage, and establish working environments that allow all to perform, to support well-being that enables optimal performance, and to provide the opportunities to learn beyond knowledge and skills, for example the ability to be resilient in times of challenge.

When and where does this matter most?

There are moments of impact every day, moments when the manager and leader have the chance to role-model, to figuratively touch the "performance wheel" and add to momentum *or* to jam up the flow and the gears. How often? Ken Blanchard and Spencer Johnson wrote *The One Minute Manager* incorporating their model of situational leadership. This is easily applied when providing context for these consequences of action.

How does the management balance sheet apply?

How many supervisors, managers, or leaders have objectives that relate to the way they fulfil their roles? How many have the behavioural application of skills acquired in achieving the most possible with and through their people? By bringing the balance sheet into play and applying it to organisation intent and purpose, you can ensure management contribution clarity.

What lies beneath?

Impact factors. Where are the stresses? Where are the dilemmas and challenges?

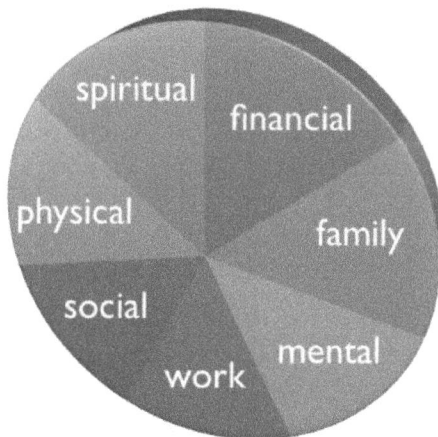

Example: Life goes beyond the workplace, and thus there are other, underlying factors to relate to the outcome and behavioural application.

Work: This includes the influence of the manager of the manager of the manager, etc., and the process v. people balance being applied from above. Other factors are pretty self-explanatory, and without prying they may all have a consequential influence over situational behaviour. These possible impactors can include financial, family, spiritual, and ethical issues.

Copyright Zig Ziglar. Used with permission.

Underlying improvement factors

These all combine to relate to any way in which capability, competencies/competence or performance drivers are collated and communicated. However, some of the example people dimensions noted below are often missed. This is not an exhaustive list but one that flags the consideration we have researched further.

Knowledge	Skill	Behaviour
People	People	People
Dominant energy	Influence	Situational consistency
Personality differences	Communication	Collaboration
All 'difference'	Handling difficult discussions	Integrating effort
Expertise – strengths	Delegation	Empowering
Fears – weaknesses	Team commitment and flow	Trust
Primary motivation factors		Living the wrap-around values

Conclusions and actions required

As stated earlier, the extent to which processes can be continually improved to meet new challenges is reducing with each change. In contrast, the value and contribution of people is increasingly becoming the most viable change and improvement lever. The role of the manager, and the measurement of how well the manager fulfils this aspect of his or her role, is key to meeting future challenges.

CHAPTER 3

POLICY AND OPERATIONS

Beyond analytics

People support in any organisation is likely to accumulate a wide range of data, some of it personal, but much of it non-sensitive information which can be used to examine various aspects of the organisation's performance and general health. The use of data from people support has progressed from metrics, the simple *measurement* of such things as staff turnover, to 'analytics', the *analysis* of data, the 'why' and the 'so what' behind the bare numbers.

However, the analysis of people-related data should not be undertaken for its own sake, in the hope that somebody, somewhere, somehow may find it interesting. Instead, *it should serve a business need*. To be relevant and worthwhile it must pass the "so what?" test.

Analysis should not be an academic exercise but a genuine attempt to address an area of relevance to the business. There is no point whatsoever in producing yet another set of figures to send to senior managers, hoping that they may somehow be able to derive some insight from it, but in the knowledge that they will probably do no more than glance at it before putting it aside. There must literally be something in it for the recipient, and for the organisation itself.

The starting point for any analysis must be a question which needs an answer, a business need which has to be addressed. The task then is to find the data which have a bearing on the need, to verify their accuracy, ensure that they are either non-sensitive or can be anonymised, and then carry out the analysis. In some cases, however, the necessary data may simply not be available.

Most organisations accumulate large quantities of data relating to their people. Length of service, pay, training undertaken, promotions, sickness absence, individual objectives—these and many more types of data are all usually available. Many of these are regularly reported on in detail, whether or not any action can be taken on them. Countless hours of staff time go into producing these numbers, but unfortunately that's so often exactly what they remain, just numbers, with little or no attempt to link them to any specific business need, or to combine them with other data to increase their value and significance.

"If we only look at analysing HR data in a silo, then there will be no business impact. We have to start showing how employee data drive relevant business outcomes .....We must do a better job of connecting people focused data to what our customers (i.e., business leaders) are focused on (business outcomes)."[1]

Getting hold of the relevant data in the first place may itself be a problem, because in many organisations the data are held in silos, with each department holding its own. This often breeds a territorial, possessive attitude among those holding the data, who come to regard the data as *theirs*, almost their personal property, leading to a reluctance to share, even with those in the same organisation. This can lead to frustrating turf wars which obstruct any effort to put the data into a wider context and gain greater benefit from them.

---

[1] Nick Holley, *Big Data and HR*, the Henley Centre for HR Excellence, Henley Business School, University of Reading (2013).

One of the authors experienced an example of this territorial behaviour while writing a strategic assessment for a large public-sector organisation. He requested data from another department, but was told the figures could not be shared because of (unspecified) "data protection reasons". In a search for proxy data to use as a substitute, he found the very data he originally requested—*on a public website!* So much for their supposed sensitivity! This was an example of an individual being obstructive because he was suspicious of the motives behind the request for "his" data, or somehow felt that the data should be used only by his department.

As the Chartered Institute for Personnel and Development (CIPD) points out: "No amount of planned and careful silo-smashing or strategic skills development on people analytics will suffice if we cannot resolve the problem of suspicion and scepticism. This cultural issue is a significant impediment to HR becoming a data-driven and analytical function."[2]

Breaking down this type of silo arrangement and the obstructive attitudes it often breeds is essential if we are to undertake analysis that is of real value to the organisation. The most valuable types of analysis involve combining different data sets, particularly adding people support data to datasets from the rest of the business. The fact that these will be held in different silos by separate departments increases the chance of encountering the kind of obstacles we have mentioned.

The CIPD identifies three main levels of analytics capability:[3]

---

[2] Chartered Institute of Personnel and Development, *Talent Analytics and Big Data: The Challenge for HR,* with the permission of the publisher, the Chartered Institute of Personnel and Development, (www.cipd.co.uk) (Nov. 2013).

[3] Chartered Institute of Personnel and Development, *HR Analytics,* with the permission of the publisher, the Chartered Institute of Personnel and Development, (May 2017), www.cipd.co.uk/knowledge/strategy/analytics/factsheet.

Level 1 – basic analytics

The use of descriptive data to illustrate an aspect of people support, for example absence or annual leave data. This involves no analysis, except for showing changes in the data over time (i.e. trends).

Level 2 – using multidimensional data

Combining different data sets, or types of data, to investigate a specific idea.

Level 3 – predictive analytics

Using people data to predict future trends. This is the most valuable type of analytics, but is the most difficult to achieve, and the least often undertaken.

Much of the data presented at Level 1 is straightforward stuff, levels of sickness absence and so on, but it is easy to overlook their importance and what they really mean. Any cyclical or seasonal fluctuations in levels of absence may reveal hidden problems in staffing levels, for example, or possibly pinch points which cause exceptional levels of stress. This can then become the trigger for more complex analysis, combining other types of data, which takes us to Level 2.

At Level 2, combining or "mashing" different types of data can sometimes throw up extremely valuable results. We mentioned earlier a situation in an organisation in which high turnover among low-paid staff was absorbing a great deal of the time of people support and line managers. A comparison of recruitment costs with the cost of a modest salary increase for the small group of staff in question might well have revealed that it would have been cheaper to increase their pay than to continually run recruitment processes when staff left for higher pay elsewhere.

Achieving Level 3, predictive analytics, is difficult, but this level of data usage offers the greatest potential value. In addition to the points made earlier in the book, using data on sales or productivity in conjunction with data on training received, for example, can help to assess the effectiveness of training and predict the likely results of future L&D efforts. Similarly, comparing recruitment levels with future retirement dates of experienced staff can pinpoint key periods when people support might need to increase recruiting efforts and concentrate on recruiting particular specialists to fill the gaps.

Predictive insight follows analysis, and when exploring the development of talent, for example, it is helpful to be able to take readings from a range of sources. What is happening to those readings already taken? Are development opportunities being taken, and if so, are they generating impact and the desired intent? Are those identified engaged, or are they at least in an engaged part of the organisation? Is their current level of performance worthy of inclusion? Where are they facing challenges, and where can you gain support? The answers to these questions require data that can be used for action to be taken within people support. They can help to predict situational blind spots and organisational needs, and can help managers to provide timely support. Thus, time devoted to analytics that help, rather than data for its own sake, is important.

We have already emphasised the need for people support to demonstrate its value to the business by aligning its activity with that of the organisation. The use of analytics, particularly of the predictive variety, offers a way to achieve this. Conversely, a people support function which produces reams of data without relating them to the needs of the business plays into the hands of its critics by reinforcing the stereotype of people support professionals who allegedly have no idea about the realities of the organisation's core activities.

"Most organisations measure too many things that don't matter, and don't put sufficient focus on those things that do, establishing a large set of metrics, but often lacking a causal mapping of the key drivers of their business."[4]

However, a survey by the CIPD in the UK has shown that many organisations have not yet started using HR analytics at all.[5] Inevitably, this tendency is most pronounced among smaller organisations. Almost half of organisations with fewer than 50 employees, and more than a quarter of those with 50 to 99,[6] reported that they do not use analytics. When it comes to *predictive* analytics, only 4 per cent of over 500 organisations in the survey were users.

In the same survey, the factors most frequently identified as barriers to the use of HR analytics were data and technology, organisation culture, and lack of analytical skills.[7]

One problem we have not yet touched upon is that of the availability of data. Organisations new to HR analytics may simply not have certain types of data available because in the past no one has seen the need to collect them. This is clearly a deal-breaker which would render analysis impossible. Even when an organisation has begun recording particular types of data, it will still take some time before there is enough to make analysis worthwhile. There is simply no easy answer to this, but it emphasises the need to think ahead and try to anticipate the questions the organisation needs to address, and then to identify the data you would need to answer them. The

---

[4] Accenture, *Analytics in Action: Breakthroughs and Barriers on the Journey to ROI* (2013).

[5] Chartered Institute of Personnel and Development, *HR Outlook, Views of Our Profession, Winter 2016–17,* with the permission of the publisher, the Chartered Institute of Personnel and Development, https://www.cipd.co.uk/Images/hr-outlook_2017_tcm18-17697.pdf.

[6] 48 per cent and 28 per cent respectively.

[7] 36 per cent, 29 per cent, and 26 per cent respectively.

positive aspect of data collection under these circumstances is that it is being undertaken for a specific reason, and not apparently for its own sake or for some obscure reason no one can explain. Anyone asking the necessity of collecting the data can thus be assured of its purpose.

The CIPD survey also identified problems with the use or distribution of HR data. We mention elsewhere that business analysts and similar staff are useful allies in the process of getting people support data in front of executives at board level, but the survey showed that among those organisations using analytics, in 56 per cent of cases *HR data and reports were not passed to data analysts*.[8] This means that in some organisations the people support specialists are taking the trouble to gather data and carry out analysis but are failing to share them with colleagues who can ensure they receive the attention of those at the very top. The CIPD survey also showed that in 46 per cent of organisations using analytics, line managers were not given access to the data either. To be honest, we struggle to understand this. Why do the difficult bit, the gathering of data and the actual analysis, and then fail to share them with other people in the organisation who could make use of them? Is this a sign of people support becoming possessive or precious about its own data, and falling victim to the silo mentality we discuss elsewhere?

As a profession we cannot afford to let this sort of attitude develop, as it will become an obstacle to our efforts to show the function's real value to the organisation. People data can have an impact on the running of the whole business and should therefore be shared as widely as possible. Data protection considerations may apply, obviously, but should never be used as an excuse, never fabricated as a means of saving us the bother of sharing data with another department. The action of putting our data in front of the

---

[8] Chartered Institute of Personnel and Development, *HR Outlook, Views of Our Profession, Winter 2016–17,* with the permission of the publisher, the Chartered Institute of Personnel and Development, (www.cipd.co.uk)

organisation's decision makers is a crucial step towards enhancing people support's reputation. Business analysts and line managers are the very people who can view people data in the context of other aspects of an organisation, and so sharing data with them is another step towards showing people support's value to the business.

To be fair, the apparent reluctance to share the results of analysis could be a symptom of people support's lack of confidence and experience in this area. It could be that, new to the whole business of analytics, people support as a function is still finding its feet and is not always confident enough to disseminate its findings to others, even within the same organisation.

A lack of confidence in our analysis must not be allowed to tempt us to distribute "raw" data, in the hope that other people may somehow be able to make better use of them than we can ourselves. Data without analysis are just numbers. Here we can again learn from the intelligence world. If you dish up raw intelligence to your customers you are likely to get one of two outcomes. Either they do nothing with it, because they don't have the time or simply don't understand what they're looking at, or else they draw their own conclusions from it, which may or may not be the right ones. Either way, you are failing the "so what?" test. The same applies to analysis in a people support context. Explain what it really means. The lessons to be learnt from any analysis should be made obvious to the recipient, as should any action to be taken in response. Is it good news, or bad? Should *they* be doing something about it, or should someone else? Don't leave them wondering, "*so what?*"

Provide insight, not spreadsheets!

Choosing certain types of data to focus on does not mean that you're somehow being less than honest by not presenting absolutely everything. One of the authors is a school governor and is regularly presented with every conceivable type of data relating to exam performance, for example, where the sheer number of trees often obscures the wood itself. Selecting the essential data and then ensuring they are presented as clearly as possible in order to illustrate the point you are making is the key to passing the "so what?" test.

"In reality, most companies don't suffer from a true Big Data problem when it comes to workforce metrics. Rather, it is mostly a lack of understanding with regard to the best metrics to track, and organising the right data and setting up processes to communicate these metrics to managers and business leaders."[9]

Exactly *how* the data are presented is just as important as the data being used. Even if you choose exactly the right data to address a particular business problem, you can still fail to get your point across if the data are not presented to best effect. The books of Edward R. Tufte, especially *The Visual Display of Quantitative Information*, provide wonderful examples of how to convey complex statistics with great clarity, even to those of us with the most acute spreadsheet phobia. For example, unless you are already an avid student of the period, a single diagram in Tufte's book will teach you more about Napoleon's invasion of Russia and the retreat from Moscow than any history book you will ever read! The same data could be presented in a spreadsheet, but one glance at them in that form would turn off 90 per cent of the people who saw it.

But history is not what we should be aiming at presenting. In any organisation, knowing how we got here is important, but knowing where we're going is even more so. Predictive analytics, the elusive Level 3 in the CIPD's classification (see above), is the type of analysis which will be most effective in proving people support's value to the organisation. However, the capacity of organisations to carry out predictive analytics is still very limited. In the Deloitte

---

[9] Holley, *Big Data and HR*, Henley Centre for HR Excellence, Henley Business School, University of Reading (2013)

2016 Global Human Capital Trends survey,[10] while 77 per cent of HR respondents viewed "people analytics" as "important" or "very important", only 8 per cent of respondents described their organisations as fully capable of developing predictive models, and 55 per cent of organisations were rated as "weak" at using HR data to predict workforce performance and improvement.

There has been much debate about whether people analytics work is best performed by people support staff who have learnt to do analysis or by analysts who have been given a grounding in people support. One of the authors is a people support person who was "reprogrammed" to enable him to carry out analysis, albeit in a non-HR context, but most people who go into people support do not do so with the intention of grappling with statistics.

The advent of more complex and sophisticated people analytics is likely to make working in or with people support more attractive to those with an analytical or statistical background, so recruiting experts in analysis who can work closely with people support specialists would seem to be a promising solution. Alternatively, being able to use some of a specialist analyst's time on people support matters, working closely with a people support specialist, would also be useful. However, these approaches will not be feasible for many organisations, particularly the smaller ones, so encouraging people support professionals to acquire some basic analysis skills would be a useful first step.

Some organisations, by their very nature, are more statistically orientated than others. Senior managers in the financial sector, or in manufacturing for example, are accustomed to being presented with complex data on the performance of the organisation, and so are likely to be particularly receptive to people data, especially where they address the problems they care about or alert them to ones they had

---

[10] Deloitte, *Global Human Capital Trends 2016: The new organization: Different by Design*, (Deloitte University Press, 2016).

not spotted themselves. But whatever the nature of the organisation, it is immensely valuable to have a "data champion", a senior figure who can speak up for the cause of analytics at board level. The champion can help to deal with the sort of situation described above, where an individual obstructs the sharing of data for spurious reasons. Having such a champion figure senior enough to be able to remove an obstacle with a single phone call or email would be an enormous boost to the prospects for implementing effective analysis.

"In the not-too-distant future, it will become impossible to make any HR decisions without analytics. Indeed, analytics capabilities will be a fundamental requirement for the effective HR business partner."[11]

The challenge of social media

"Why do social media sites like LinkedIn appear to know more about my employees than we do, and how can we leverage these data and insights?"[12]

The growth in popularity of social media has placed online a mass of material on individuals, including their work skills, qualifications, and knowledge, together with their attitudes and intentions. This information, input, verified and maintained by the individuals themselves, is often more comprehensive, accurate, and up to date than the information on those same employees held on people support systems. As a result, it represents a hugely valuable, and often untapped, source of information which can be used by people support.

Despite the value to people support of social media data, only 5 per cent of companies surveyed by Deloitte in 2015 considered

---

[11] Deloitte, *Global Human Capital Trends 2016: The new organization: Different by Design*, (Deloitte University Press, 2016).
[12] Deloitte, *Global Human Capital Trends 2015: Leading in the new world of work* (Deloitte University Press, 2015).

their policy for using such data to be "excellent", and 81 per cent said they were either "not ready" or only "somewhat ready" to take advantage of it.[13]

Data from social media can be used both in the selection of candidates for job interviews and in determining the views of existing employees. Several start-ups monitor data from social networking sites to try to predict employees' intentions regarding applying for jobs outside the company. These companies claim that their data provide a better predictor of flight risk than any internal data held by the employer.[14] This form of "retention prediction" and "sentiment analysis" appears likely to grow in popularity in the future as firms seek to develop internal talent to cope with skill shortages among external candidates.

Conclusion

People-related analytics can reveal organisation-wide problems, and in doing so prove the value of people support to the business, but must still pass the "so what?" test. As we explained above, the analysis of people data should be undertaken as a means of trying to answer a specific business-related question. It should never be undertaken simply for its own sake, or just in the hope that an addressee may find a use for the results.

We need to take care when it comes to the form in which data are presented. Distributing raw data, without analysis, risks either inaction or possibly the wrong action from the recipients. Relatively few people are turned on by acres of spreadsheets, and an effective presentation of the data can make all the difference in the recipient's response. However, pretty is not necessarily the same as effective, and clarity is paramount.

---

[13] Ibid.
[14] Ibid.

The most valuable forms of analytics will be those which involve combining datasets to predict future developments. This type of analysis can sometimes identify the precious "unknown unknowns"', the Holy Grail of both the intelligence world and people support, those trends or problems which no one notices until they suddenly appear out of the woodwork and cause a "Why didn't we see that coming?" situation. Developing the ability to see over the horizon in this way and prevent the organisation from being caught out by unexpected problems would clearly enhance people support's reputation and help show its true value to the business.

Having a senior figure as 'data champion' within the organisation is invaluable to remove the barriers created when you are faced by the silo mentality of people who become possessive over data for which they are responsible.

Overshadowing and endangering all these good intentions, however, is the shortage of analytical skills among people support professionals. Some understanding of analytics will in any case be increasingly necessary in the near future for people support specialists, simply in order to interpret data to make decisions on people matters, and so developing the ability to carry out the analysis itself is a logical further step. Those of us with a learning and development background have spent years telling other people to overcome inertia and fear of the unknown in order to learn new skills, so perhaps it behoves *us* now to accept the need to embrace analytical skills as part and parcel of proactive people support work.

Having explored the way in which analytics need to be part of your policy, and embedded within people support and development to enable forward-thinking action, we will now briefly consider some of the traditional policies, and whether you could ensure they better align to your unique purpose and intent.

CHAPTER 4

BEYOND REWARD

Since Dan Pink wrote his book *Drive*, in which he identified the myths relating to reward and performance, the challenges associated with pay, reward, entitlement, bonuses, equality, and more have all risen to the front of change thinking.

The link with organisation design is not always highlighted, and we have found most organisations operating the functions independently. For meeting current and future challenges, we recommend the bringing together of these considerations.

Each function, the balance of roles within it, and the individual job design relate to the expected value these things generate. Pink recommends that except for "if this-then that" jobs, the salaries reflect the expected value, that is, they take the issue of pay off the table.

The underlying organisation design principles and considerations of finance, process, people, and customer experience need to be applied to strategic intent. Within them are the art and science behind job design and expected value.

So, what are the immediate challenges that need to be considered within this context?

Gender pay gap challenge

HR Magazine noted that from April, "Firms will need to start recording data to report on their gender pay gap in 2018."[1] However, some have argued that this will not give an accurate picture of the problem. So, will reporting the gender pay gap lead to any problems, and what could firms do to counter them?

When we looked at alternatives for job sizing and pay range, we felt that the solution as noted would be gender-neutral, that is that you pay for the role, not the person, and that people are rewarded for contribution, not for reputation. This is not easy. Entitlement and "getting a great deal" are drivers for individuals. Businesses are falling for the "this is the only person" trap. The market is full. To take a "right person at the right pay in the right way" approach will, over time, address things.

Is the gender pay gap purely that? Well, the BBC has some challenges. The uproar that followed the release of salaries and pay levels in 2017 has shown the folly of that thought in so many ways. Why does it matter, and where is the real problem? It matters because it is the licence payers' money. On the second question, it is not the gender pay gap. Although annoying, this is the result, not the cause. It is the mindsets of those who deemed it appropriate and acceptable to pay certain individuals so highly. What lies behind that? Is it fear of headlines relating to being unable to hold onto such people, or fear of internal politics, or a genuine belief that these are extraordinary talents? We would ask the BBC to sit down and give real thought to what constitutes talent. If it is someone who cannot be replaced, then the pay levels may possibly be justified. However, one would objectively ask, is this person really irreplaceable?

---

[1] Carole Easton and Maggie Stilwell, "Hot topic: Gender pay gap reporting", *HR Magazine* (Apr. 2017).

There has been much written on the gender pay gap. This is a fact, if taken on the evidence comparing those at the highest levels in an organisational hierarchy. We do not have the evidence of those being paid "normal" salaries, so the headlines are not necessarily true throughout all levels. We don't know. In this specific instance, there are two ways to bring the gender payments more in line. One of these ways does not increase the pay for the female celebrities but does recalibrate the salaries being paid to the male "stars". Ideally it would be about a realistic pay level for all. Recognising and calculating the value that each individual adds would be a start. It is the unbelievable levels of the few that should be reconsidered. Be brave: would you really miss them? Are they "irreplaceable"? Are they outstanding in their field?

Such irresponsible pay offers, potentially based upon fear of losing individuals, are not the restricted domain of the BBC; they happen in many industries. For example, there was and is a similar feel in investment banking and, to some degree, in the increasing gap between the pay levels of executives and staff. Contracts which allow for the reward of failure, or at least not meeting expectations, are often negotiated. Is it time to stand up and just pass? There are many examples of the executive merry-go-round attracting individuals at ever increasing pay levels who are not the only people able to make a difference. Some may not be making the difference that the PR department has portrayed. One of the authors wrote recently about the management balance sheet where net value is identified. Perhaps we could extend the use beyond managing performance and into recruitment and the reward of talent.

While making comment and focusing on the BBC, allow us to state that the lack of spend control does not rest with pay levels. Just look at the way in which weather and business news presenters travel the country. Or the overuse of past performers in athletics coverage and other sports. They often appear more important than the action. Back to talent, then: clearly very good in their day, yet less so in this role. There are so many being paid to utter platitudes and offer much less insight than the airtime would suggest their pay levels warrant.

The established practices could be reversed.

I would ask that the response from the BBC to the claims of the celebrity women be thought through and viewed from the other end of the telescope, as noted earlier. Call the bluff of those perceived as being paid extravagantly, and seek people who can be professional and deliver higher levels of skill for less. Extend such reviews to the sheer number of people being paid at high levels to add nothing.

The world of celebrity should get real. When celebrities are earning many times more than the Prime Minister, then the level of decision-making complexity or the quality of delivery and skill levels being used must be significantly higher to justify the rewards.

Equality should be consistently and fairly applied for the right reasons in the right way and in the right context, without bias or discrimination in any form. It is not simply about ticking equality boxes: it is about doing the right thing in every situation in ways that can be easily understood.

However, if we see it as a genuine challenge at all levels, then why? Given the length of time equality and diversity legislation has been in place, one would have hoped for better. Maggie Stilwell, managing partner for talent, EY UK & Ireland, has stated, "One of the greatest challenges surrounding the topic is the confusion between pay gap and equal pay. Greater clarity is needed to educate and inform on the difference between the two, which is often misunderstood."[2]

---

[2] Carole Easton and Maggie Stilwell, "Hot topic: Gender pay gap reporting", *HR Magazine* (Apr. 2017).

In this context, what are the causes? Olivia Mitchell, the director of the Pension Research Council at the Wharton School of the University of Pennsylvania, has identified three key causal factors.[3] The third is that of employer bias. However, we will incorporate it slightly differently when exploring her first two causes, below.

The motherhood penalty

Research identified that many mothers suffer workplace-related consequences after having a child.[4]

Mothers suffer a penalty relative to non-mothers and men, in the form of lower perceived competence and commitment, higher professional expectations, lower likelihood of hiring and promotion, and lower recommended salaries. This evidence implies that being a mother leads to discrimination in the workplace. Is it actual discrimination, or possibly unconscious bias? This is something for which there has been an increase in training demand in the past two years. The cause-and-effect factors are rarely explored. If we take the straight data noted below, then it is a huge issue.

- For women, competency ratings were 10 per cent lower for mothers compared to non-mothers among otherwise equal candidates.

- Mothers were 12.1 percentage points less committed to their jobs than non-mothers, whereas fathers were perceived as being 5 percentage points more committed

---

[3] Madeline Farber, "3 Reasons Why the Gender Pay Gap Still Exists," *Fortune* (Apr. 2017).
[4] Shelley J. Correll, Stephen Benard, and In Paik, "Getting a Job: Is There a Motherhood Penalty?" *American Journal of Sociology*, 112/5 (2007), 1297–1339, retrieved from Harvard Kennedy School Women and Public Policy Program's Gender Action portal, http://gap.hks.harvard.edu/getting-job-there-motherhood-penalty.

than non-fathers. Compared to childless men, mothers were rated 6.4 percentage points lower regarding commitment.

- Mothers were 6 times less likely than childless women and 3.35 times less likely than childless men to be recommended for hire. Similarly, mothers are also disadvantaged when it comes to promotions. Childless women are 8.2 times more likely to be recommended for a promotion than mothers. In the audit study conducted with real employers, childless women still have an advantage. They receive 2.1 times as many callbacks as equally qualified mothers.

- Mothers were also held to higher punctuality standards than non-mothers. On average, mothers could be late 3.16 days per month before no longer being recommended for hire, whereas childless women could be late on 3.73 days. Conversely, fathers could have more days late than non-fathers: 3.6 days per month compared to 3.16 days.

- Mothers were recommended a 7.9 per cent lower starting salary than non-mothers ($139,000 compared to $151,000 respectively), which is 8.6 per cent lower than the recommended starting salary for fathers. Among men, the trend is reversed, and fathers were offered a significantly higher starting salary than childless men ($152,000 compared to $148,000 respectively).

So often, there is a two-way issue. Unconscious bias is fed by unconscious action on the part of others. It is worthwhile to look at how coaching for return to work has made significant differences in organisations that have been bold enough to anticipate the niggling issue. In Sweden, subsidised day care has gone some way towards alleviating some of these problems. However, given that problems occur with potential unconscious bias, awareness of the issue and acceptance of its potential for disruption are the first steps.

Negotiation challenge

Hannah Riley Bowles notes that the problem may have more to do with how women are treated when they negotiate than with their general confidence or skills at negotiation—as she refers to it, the "social cost" of negotiation.[5] Again, there is an element of potential unconscious bias, and also the unconscious dismissal of the value of contribution. The extension of the two-way support and development activity mentioned above would help, as would training in negotiation or in preparing for and managing difficult or stressful discussions. By going beyond the headline, getting deeper insight, and communicating positively, those within people support can coordinate proactive supportive frameworks that quietly start to move the issue off the table.

Picking up on the bias aspect, Madeline Farber notes, "Negative, deeply rooted stereotypes about women's abilities and opportunities are at the root of gender discrimination, perpetuating societal issues like pay disparity, occupational segregation and fewer leadership opportunities."[6]

She adds that other causes of the gender pay gap beyond the three above include women typically being overrepresented in lower-paying fields. However, there are more factors to overlay here, such as immigration, educational equality, and situational significance. Carole Easton, CEO of Young Women's Trust, adds, "Pay transparency alone will not change the gender stereotypes that often determine the types of roles men and women take and the industries they work in. We need action to support young women into male-dominated areas if we are to close the gender pay gap."[7]

---

[5] Hannah Riley Bowles, *Why Women Don't Negotiate Their Job Offers*, *Harvard Business Review* (19 June 2014).

[6] Farber, *3 Reasons Why the Gender Pay Gap Still Exists*.

[7] Easton and Stilwell, *Hot Topic* (HR Magazine, April 2017).

It is, however, the skills and perceived value of contribution that matter. When adding wider issues such as work–life balance, the reverse may also be relevant.

Yet, again, is it the core issue? Kate Whelan, director of reward and HR services, Telefonica UK, reflects, "Will it [gender pay reporting] create undue focus on a single digit with companies being placed in league tables? Hours will be spent gathering data, calculating trends, manipulating statistics to tell a better story and move up the league table. Time that would be better spent addressing the root cause." Rather than focusing on gender pay differences we should be looking at gender balance."[8]

This moves us closer to our suggestion that we need to look at data that matter, data that can enable difference, and data that can enable change. The quality of that data analysis and the facilitation of action that follows can help to shift unconscious or even deeply rooted bias. It is the *why* that can drive the change, the *what* that informs and convinces, and the opportunity to refocus the ways we attempt to do this—going beyond training to facilitated support and focused impact.

The reporting itself will not change things. There is a deeper challenge, one that people support should grab hold of and take the lead on. With strong leadership, the bias and fairness, injustices and irreconcilable gaps, can be addressed quickly. Using the job design, the context of expected value and creative reward, the gap and the issue of equality can be tackled at pace. With the taking of responsibility and the creation of appropriate salaries for the value return expected, the issue can be taken off the table and unnecessary costs associated with "reporting" taken away.

---

[8] Kathryn Clapp and Kate Whelan, "Hot topic: Gender pay gap reporting, part two", *HR Magazine* (Apr. 2017).

Executive pay challenges

The gap between staff and executive pay has exploded. As an issue, it was one of the first statements that Theresa May made on becoming UK Prime Minister. People support, as HR, has essentially played the role of a bystander throughout the last two decades, almost voyeuristic in the way it has pampered to demands. The same was true in banking on the subject of bonuses. The argument has been that if you don't pay, then you don't get or keep the talent. Essentially, no one really took up the challenge. Was talent so thin on the ground? Were the results being obtained worth that level of reward? The financial crisis in recent years is, in part, attributed to the way executives are rewarded. The Financial Services Authority considered that remuneration practices were a "contributory factor to the market crisis".[9] To manage this in the future, the EU's Capital Requirements Directive, CRD IV, requires that bonuses in the finance sector be limited to 100 per cent of base pay, or 200 per cent with the approval of at least 66 per cent of shareholders.[10] The reported multi- million pound bonuses paid to banking executives who have subsequently "moved on" amid regulatory questions was an extreme example, yet who asked the questions?

More recently, in 2016, the man in charge of Southern Rail, with whom we associate delays, cancellations, and strike action, was paid £495,000. The company reported a pretax loss of more than £15 million on turnover of £1.1 billion for the year ending 2 July 2016. In contrast, David Brown, the chief executive of Go-Ahead, the parent company, refused an annual bonus and pay increase. The submitted annual report states: "The directors' remuneration policy is designed to reflect the group's performance, with elements of remuneration linked to our strategic priorities, particularly

---

[9] Financial Services Authority, *A regulatory response to the global banking crisis*, Discussion Paper 9/2 (Mar. 2009).

[10] Linklaters, *European Parliament votes on CRD IV, Including Bonus Cap* (Apr. 2013).

health and safety, customer satisfaction, and operating profit and cashflow."

The impact of the gap is a significant one. CIPD research has revealed that the disproportionate level of CEO pay is a huge issue for employees, with 59 per cent of employees citing it as a reason they are demotivated at work.[11]

The government's Green Paper published in November 2016[12] includes proposals that will:

- force companies to publish pay ratios that show the difference in earning between the chief executive and average employee;
- improve the effectiveness of remuneration committees and the extent to which they must consult shareholders and the wider company on pay;
- introduce binding votes on executive pay packages.

Speaking to the House of Commons, Business Secretary Greg Clark noted, "This government is unequivocally and unashamedly pro-business, but we hold business to a high standard in doing so."[13] Theresa May previously raised the prospect of placing employee representatives on boards during her Conservative leadership campaign over the summer, but has since told businesses she will not make them do so. Many have them anyway, but our research into this has demonstrated little training for the representatives and a reticence to question.

[11] Chartered Institute of Personnel and Development, *CIPD welcomes first steps in repairing UK's broken executive pay system*, with the permission of the publisher, the Chartered Institute of Personnel and Development (Nov. 2016), https://www.cipd.co.uk/about/media/press/repairing-executive-pay-system.
[12] Department for Business, Energy, and Industrial Strategy, *Corporate Governance Reform: Green Paper* (Nov. 2016).
[13] Zlata Rodionova, "Theresa May could force companies to reveal pay gap between executives and average workers", *The Independent* (29 Nov. 2016).

What does that mean to those within people support?

It is the breaking of habit that is our challenge, going beyond the current communities of influence and hidden relationships to explore the considerations of every individual.

What motivates?

As noted earlier, the work of Dan Pink in his book *Drive* has opened the subject of how to relate financial incentive to performance and whether you are paying the person, the role, or both, in context of the other, to make the expected contribution. To pay bonuses or not? What is the full range of mini rewards for excellence? What is valued by employees as a perk and something that is worth having?

Bonuses were virtually unknown to employees across most of UK business before the 1980s.

Since that time, has management improved? There are so many stories of demotivation from the process behind the issue of bonuses, whether related to appraisals and forced distribution curves or not. One less-than-positive effect of a bonus regime is the reinforcement of "them and us" with senior managers and directors, along with people support, secretly impacting the lives of employees, assuming their hierarchical position to incorporate potentially unconscious bias within decisions. When one of the authors worked in banking, there was a strongly held belief that the process was fundamentally flawed yet hiding behind apparent "best practice". If not really working, then by definition it is not even good practice.

Bonuses granted to executives and senior employees in the industry at that time were perceived as excessive by many. Articles referred to 'executive greed.' Beyond the issue was the belief that to recruit the best you needed to offer rewards in excess of the market and that only those being recruited were able to deliver the expected intent and value. Those being recruited were able to almost dictate terms. But were they really the ONLY people capable of delivering value?

Kathleen O'Donnell in *Off the Cusp*[14] notes, though specifically relating to dentistry practices, that bonuses can in some circumstances be an effective motivational tool that can result in increased production and collections, and make team members operate like stakeholders in the practice. Dan Pink relates the potential in "if-then"-type roles. However, a bonus programme alone won't fix or override other problems that may exist, and can intensify some issues at times, resulting in demotivating the team. One suggestion she makes is to pay out not monthly but more sporadically throughout the year, which would prevent team members from relying on the bonus and making financial commitments that they could not afford without a bonus.

In the CIPD fact sheet[15] on bonuses, they identify a trend to incorporate bonus and incentive plans into reward packages. This has been driven in part by the influence of the new pay philosophy which advocates that guaranteed basic pay should comprise a small element of the overall reward package, and a shift towards strategic reward linking employee performance and pay to the wider business strategy.

Relating relevance, simplicity, and *perceived value* against costs, potential impact of greater than expected performance, and the consistency of application will help determine whether bonuses have a place in your reward packages. Following this is the need to consider detail.

Again, the order of the following key questions is important. If management can jump to the answer, can solutioneer, then the consequences and impact will not have been fully explored. The questions include:

---

[14] Kathleen O'Donnell, "Bonuses—the Good and the Bad", *Off the Cusp* (6 Mar. 2014).

[15] Chartered Institute of Personnel and Development, *Bonuses and Incentives: Learn How to Design and Operate an Effective Bonus or Incentive Scheme* (1 Mar. 2016), with the permission of the publisher, the Chartered Institute of Personnel and Development https://www.cipd.co.uk/knowledge/fundamentals/people/pay/bonuses-factsheet.

1. Why do we need bonuses? Why do we need to do more than provide salary?

2. What are we hoping to achieve? What is not happening now? What needs to change?

3. Who is involved? Who will manage any decisions? Who will be affected?

4. Where are the issues most prevalent? Where will bonuses make the biggest difference?

5. When should bonuses be paid?

6. How should bonuses be compiled, managed, and implemented? How simple can they be? How can all track them. That is, how transparent will they be?

As the CIPD fact sheet advises, "If they are to impact on employee behaviour or performance, bonus or incentive payments need to be 'worth having', that is, set at a sufficiently high level to have an effect. By contrast, caution needs to be taken in setting bonuses at very high levels to avoid driving undesired behaviours or outcomes, such as the crowding out of non-financial motivation."[16]

People support has a major challenge in overcoming a feeling of entitlement, of policing the rigour and principles behind schemes, ensuring consistent and unbiased application, ensuring the alignment to the organisation's intent and purpose, and the creation of value worthy of additional payment.

---

[16] Chartered Institute of Personnel and Development, *Bonuses and Incentives: Learn How to Design and Operate an Effective Bonus or Incentive Scheme* (1 Mar. 2016), with the permission of the publisher, the Chartered Institute of Personnel and Development https://www.cipd.co.uk/knowledge/fundamentals/people/pay/bonuses-factsheet.

Non-cash incentive schemes, based on the receipt of a gift or prize, are increasing in use, and are seen as memorable, exciting, and having impact. Ad hoc rewards, as highlighted with Leon Restaurants, or beyond this, selected incentives such as Perkbox, inspire a pride in the company intent. These can be more cost-efficient for the organisation.

In customer-facing industries, non-cash incentive schemes may be based on the use of a single prize to be won by the highest-performing individual employee or qualifying employees, or encompass a range of awards recognising different levels of achievement.

The challenge of legislation—funding the bill

As referenced and alluded to earlier, people support would appear to be having less influence over the consequential thinking relating to legislation This is especially true in terms of small business, yet not exclusively. The apprentice levy and the minimum or living wage adds strain on even larger businesses.

A case study—Leon Restaurants

When we interviewed Marco Reick, the people director of Leon Restaurants, he explained how the levy is essentially an unnecessary and restrictive piece of legislation. Far from creating opportunities, it is reducing them. It reminds him of the Holy Roman Empire—"neither Holy, nor Roman, nor ..." Regulation consequences need to be managed and certainly add costs. Leon Restaurants is an expanding and growing business with unique levers. Their purpose is to help everyone to live and eat well.

The consequences of increased costs impact the company's biggest challenge, which is culture. The challenges for people support are to continue finding ways to support people to deliver their purpose and continually improve the way they do so—to do what makes a difference and to help with their focus. Do they stop or outsource lower-value actions? There is a lot of effort applied to internal communications and the well-being of staff, with team surveys to ensure involvement and individual departments getting net promoter scores on service provided to colleagues.

Specific and immediate challenges include:

- the living wage and apprentice levy
- Brexit
- food prices
- rates.

Having said this, we note that the first two challenges have team turnover as an underlying issue. The levels of productivity and customer impact (average spend per customer) are much higher for existing staff than for new starters. After six months there is an increase, then the longer the employee stays, there is a definitive improved level of service and value.

In the current workforce (May 2017), 62 per cent of individuals come from the European Union and 25 per cent of the revenue goes to labour costs. Recruitment is a challenge. There is a reliance on the EU and free movement, and since the Brexit vote the number of applications has reduced by 20 per cent. There is a need to be creative with recruitment. Industries such as hospitality need new ponds to fish

There is a danger that increased costs could mean that firms lose funding to create the jobs in the first place. The impact on costs of the apprentice levy and the consequences of Brexit are substantial. Companies such as Leon Restaurants will need to save costs elsewhere. Potentially there may need to be more automated processes with less customer service—contrary to their intent. Leon has three priorities for the company:

1. sales
2. cost of sales
3. turnover of people.

To meet these priorities, the directors, especially founder John Vincent and People Director Marco Reick, are supporters of the type of culture and working environment that Herb Kelleher created at Southwest Airlines. They have internal job titles; for example, Marco's is "action man". The following four quotes attributed to Kelleher provide an insight into the kind of culture intended:

- "Power should be reserved for weightlifting and boats, and leadership really involves responsibility."
- "A company is stronger if it is bound by love rather than by fear."
- "We will hire someone with less experience, less education, and less expertise, over someone who has more of those things and has a rotten attitude. Because we can train people, we teach people how to lead. We can teach people how to provide customer service. But we can't change their DNA." This was fully picked up by Rita Bailey with the creative training team.
- "One piece of advice that always stuck in my mind is that people should be respected and trusted as people, not because of their position or title."

In 2017, aviation was the "Leaders of Leon" theme. Some of the outputs and underlying actions include the promotion of "live well, eat well". The motivational sessions include exploring the unwritten rules and how to learn them. Every meeting starts with "Glimpses of Brilliance", notes taken from the restaurant *Glimpses of Brilliance* book. They contribute to the family *Glimpses of Brilliance* book.

The organisation is trying new things, for example the singing restaurant in Theatreland. This could possibly develop further to include recordings or productions. They have explored sessions with

Guy Hirst on *Risky Business* and retained Martin Bromley as an advisor. Stories help to bring focus to what matters.

It is still a young and dynamic organisation and has "wrap-around values" that form the basis for their culture. They are:

- Be kind.
- Be a leader.
- Live and eat well.

The CFO is on board, helped no doubt by Leon's just having had their first £1 million "Eat Well Day".

With a commercial outlook, the efforts to influence culture and results are given context. Four actions that are driving such thinking are:

1. **Centralised induction (four per month) with a highly skilled trainer.**
   Leon Restaurants have recognised the "big school" feeling of the first few days in a restaurant. They need a positive feeling. All those completing the induction receive a John Lewis food-related gift such as a kitchen range oven mitts. Early output is up.

2. **Restaurants and head office have flexible working, genuine flexible working.**
   Part time is set to suit the individual, for example, an early shift of 7–11 or, for a single mother, 10–2 or 11–3. Some can do later and early, as in first thing and last thing, to release the core of the day for children or something similar. They see no need to stick rigidly to shift patterns and have local resource management. There is a job to be done, and local managers are trusted to deliver it. Marco Reick was on a recent conference panel with larger organisations. He saw that they are giving flexibility in an inflexible way!

3. **The intended impact grid link is strong.**
   It all relates back to convenient healthy eating as a purpose. Well-being is important, and meetings start with stretching and breathing exercises, readying participants to commit the time and to achieve glimpses of brilliance. Time is devoted to educating on diet and "good food".

4. **Bonuses are personal and team-driven.**
   They are personal and company-wide in nature and are output-driven by role. The hourly paid staff can add £1 per hour on the "big 5 measures" relating to customer feedback. They are simple, understandable, and achievable. For restaurant managers, the bonus relates to the "big 5-plus" team turnover (individual by restaurant) plus budget over achievement (they propose their own budget, which is reviewed and agreed upon), and they earn up to 20 per cent of their annual salary. In the head office, company targets are fed with a functional net promoter score, general income, and three to six role-related personal objectives.

We have explored beyond the simple impact of the legislation with this Leon case study because, fundamentally, legislation costs are likely to impact not just upon customer service but also upon the culture intended. Given that the company sees this as a competitive advantage, their intent is to create a positive working environment and customer experience and add to general well-being. The unintended costs of poor legislation will go beyond financial cost.

The government has recently announced a six-month review of modern working practices, and HMRC is setting up a new unit, the Employment Status and Intermediaries Team, to investigate firms. However, where is the issue and what is the focus of the potential consequences of action?

The decision that leaders who hosted Weight Watchers meetings were employees for PAYE and National Insurance contributions purposes was different. The organisation was structured to ensure a degree of control by the sales division, and this was sufficient to evidence an employment relationship, despite a clause in the documentation that the leaders had absolute discretion as to how classes were conducted. In the hearing, the judgement noted that this "did not reflect the practical reality of the relationship".[17]

If you closely control how, when and where a person works, if you insist on having that person working for you rather than a replacement, you may be their employer with all the tax and legal implications. Current interpretation of employment law in the UK means that if you use self-employed people or independent contractors, you will need to ensure that paperwork reflects their reality, and that any third-party supplier (optional provider) can demonstrate they are the replacement provider and are trusted in this capacity. These are real challenges in terms of letting go and ensuring you work with those you can trust to deliver consistent quality for your organisation.

The challenge of perception—the link to fairness

As mentioned elsewhere, the perceived fairness of employee rewards (or the lack thereof) is often the root of why employees leave organisations. The level of demotivation of perceived unfair or irrelevant meetings in organisations can be at times sensed. Productivity levels can dip, a negative impact on the paid-for expectations of the role can be seen, and general engagement levels can be deeply affected. The "negative wiring", as described by Lynda Gratton, becomes prevalent.

---

[17] Ernst and Young, Employment Tax Alert, *Weight Watchers—Employment Status* (2011).

CIPD research[18] demonstrates that employees' perception of fairness and equitable treatment is a core driver of retention, engagement, and performance. They relate three types of fairness in the workplace. The first, distributive, relates to equity versus equality in rewards. It may not be equal, but it must be logical. The second is procedural, and relates to a fair or consistent reward process. Perception is key. Finally is interactional, relating to the need for interactions, for example performance management meetings, that reinforce what the employee observes.

Employees will compare fairness relative to others, such as the supervisor and subordinates, peers doing the same job and similar jobs in the organisation, and peers in other organisations.[19] Fairness is a primary need for the brain and is highly correlated to trust, which is the key to unlocking engagement and performance. Studies show that people are willing to forgo personal gain to prevent others from getting what is perceived as an inequitable outcome. In the workplace, retaliation to injustice often takes the form of silent acts that directly affect the other person, such as refusing to help the offending colleague or finishing the work more slowly. Transparency in how decisions are made will go a long way towards supporting fairness and trust.[20]

The CIPD have completed research into the changing contours of fairness that highlights new work challenges.[21]

The results are interesting in the context of pay and reward. It is a significant challenge. Fairness is, as with most people-related

---

[18] Chartered Institute of Personnel and Development, *The Changing Contours of Fairness* (4 Nov. 2013), with the permission of the publisher, the Chartered Institute of Personnel and Development (www.cipd.co.uk).

[19] Chris Ceplenski, "Employee Rewards: The Importance of Perceived Fairness", *HR Daily Advisor* (June 2013).

[20] Susanne Jacobs, "Why "fairness" affects staff performance", *People Management* (Aug. 2013).

[21] Ibid.

issues, unique to your organisation. In meeting the need for reward to impact positively, people support must create it for your organisation. Strong people support is again needed and must address the reality of your organisation.

Table 1: What do employees see as unfair?	
Triggers of Unfairness	**Percentage of 'unfair' events**
Pay (freeze, long hours, senior management pay/ bonuses, differences in pay)	20
Workload (distribution)	11
Bullying/ discrimination/ harassment	11
Favouritism	10
Forced redundancy/ redundancy procedures	10
Promotion decisions	8
Flexible work (as it relates to task, time, and so on)	4
Performance review system/ appraisal	4
Pension decisions/ Schemes	4
Changes in employment terms and conditions	3
Age/ gender/ disability discrimination	3
Unfair dismissal	2
Respect	2
Lack of voice	2
Disciplinary procedures/ actions	1
Work hours	1
Job downgrades with larger role size	1
Reward system	1

The challenge of the gig economy

Portfolio careers are on the rise. This is the combining of two or three jobs or specialisms to enable a balanced and varied workload, with the added benefit that if you lose one job or choose to lose a job, you'll still have other sources of income. Initially, these were developed out of necessity, but now more by choice. This practice may even involve a degree of job sharing.

The challenges to people support regarding the reality of the new working environment are many. Legislation is unhelpful when it assumes a single picture of the workplace and working patterns. The biggest assumption is that portfolio working is for the old, when one has given up on a focused career and is preparing to hand over to a younger generation. In the world of linear progression—learn,

earn, return—the appropriate stage for portfolios is late life. But if living for a hundred years and working productively for the greater part of that will soon be a reality, as argue London Business School professors Lynda Gratton and Andrew Scott in *The 100-Year Life*, then associated challenges to people support will also be accelerated.

These are challenges that, strategically, all people support needs to refocus in order to go beyond the current work structures, to go beyond existing performance expectations and examine ways in which market considerations will be met and what role *people* will have in doing this. Automation *is* a challenge. Where will people add value? To do so, what will be needed in terms of people support and development? Who is responsible?

To return to another common theme that can continue to be applied, when being paid to do something for someone, every individual is responsible for their performance, for their own development, and for the contribution and development of others they are working with, to achieve the intent. Keeping this in the context of change, transformation and challenges will help us to steer through them.

CHAPTER 5

EMPLOYEE RELATIONS

Employee relations is the term which has come to replace industrial relations. It is part of the spectrum of activity which also includes engagement, but in this case it moves into the more official or formal areas of relations with trade unions and compliance with the law. There is therefore a defensive element to it, designed to avoid disputes, preserve reputation, and, as a bottom line, keep management out of court.

However, employee relations is seen as embracing both collective and individual workplace relationships, with a recent focus on individual well-being and work–life balance. This has proved itself to be not just superficial "touchy-feeliness", but a range of activities which have been shown to have a measurable benefit to an organisation's bottom line.

Both of the authors grew up in an era of turbulent industrial relations, with the term "collective bargaining" cropping up in the news almost nightly. At that time (the 1960s and '70s) this usually referred to agreements involving huge firms employing thousands of staff, or often to entire industries. In 1980, more than three-quarters of the UK workforce was covered by collective agreements, but by 2000, they applied to less than a third.

Today, most union officials spend their time dealing with individual cases, so the approach is very different. In addition, union membership, especially in private-sector organisations, has declined considerably over recent decades, and the individual aspect of disputes is now at the forefront of employee relations.

The increasing focus on the individual's relationship with line managers and the organisation as a whole, and on personal well-being, has led to a closer examination of the impact of these factors on the organisation's performance.

The importance of individual well-being has become a bit of an elephant-in-the-room subject, in that it has been widely acknowledged to have a clear, positive link with organisational performance, and yet many organisations are failing to make it a priority or to adopt measures to promote it. In the CIPD 2015 Absence Management Survey in the UK, 57 per cent of respondents reported that employee well-being was taken into consideration in business decisions either "to a little extent" or "not at all", while only 8 per cent of employers had a stand-alone well-being strategy. The 2015 Edenred-Ipsos Well-being Barometer found that virtually all employers (97 per cent) were convinced of the link between employee well-being and organisational performance, and yet only 26 per cent reported that they regarded well-being as a priority.

Employee voice and social media

Employee voice, the ability of employees to literally have a say in decisions affecting their work, has long been acknowledged to encourage engagement.

Many organisations are using enterprise social networks (ESNs in HR-speak) to enable employees to express opinions. These are in-house social media networks through which employees can both raise ideas with line managers and discuss matters with their colleagues, and do so in more or less real time. These systems enable rapid communication in a rather more informal manner than might otherwise be possible. Informal it may be, but it has the ability to get a point across quickly and concisely, and to gather agreement and confirmation from colleagues equally quickly. It is no wonder the CIPD has described this type of communication as "voice with muscle".[1]

Such a channel is ideal for employees who work in different departments, on widely scattered sites or on shifts whereby they seldom meet their colleagues. One of the authors once managed a team in the pre-email era who were spread over five sites, making communication within the team extremely difficult. The ability to communicate across the whole team as rapidly and as effectively as this would have been invaluable.

The informality of social-media-type systems is particularly helpful in encouraging younger employees, or those of any age in the more junior posts and who may be reticent about approaching managers, to comment on topics relating to their work. The immediacy of this approach, and the fact that it is continuously available, offers far more encouragement to participate than the familiar annual staff survey, about which many people are extremely cynical. The importance of the speed of feedback provided by social media is obvious: "Why would you wait months to understand the mood of your employees, when in just a few seconds you can understand reactions to what is happening, not what has happened?"[2]

---

[1] Chartered Institute of Personnel and Development, *Social media and employee voice: the current landscape*, (2013), with the permission of the publisher, the Chartered Institute of Personnel and Development social-media-and-employee-voice_2013-current-landscape-sop_tcm18-10327.pdf.

[2] "What is leadership?: In the HR hot seat", *HR Magazine*. Weblog post available at http://content.yudu.com/Library/A1uvje/ HRMagazineDecember20/resources/17.htm.

Using social media as an internal communications channel in this way also allows managers to tap into the "folk memory" of their organisation, to get answers to questions of the "Does anyone remember what we did last time?" variety. It also enables a sort of crowdsourcing approach to problem solving, whereby business-related matters can be discussed among the employees concerned, and ideas exchanged, all in more or less real time.

However, we must not allow an enthusiastic rush to adopt new technology to leave some employees behind. It is important to acknowledge that not everyone is an avid user of Facebook, Twitter, or other social media platforms, and so there must still be alternative communication channels available for those who prefer more traditional methods. At the very least, organisations should be prepared to offer training to any employees who need it. It is all too easy to overlook training needs and to assume that everyone is already up to speed with popular digital media. One of the authors worked for a large public-sector organisation when it introduced internet access and email for all employees. Management simultaneously adopted email as its principal method of internal communication, but many older staff, in particular, simply had little or no experience in using it, and were reluctant to constantly ask colleagues for help. No training was available, and consequently many people were slow in adopting this medium.

As it happens, despite the fact that digital media are very much the "flavour of the month", a recent survey has shown that more traditional methods are still frequently used and are still viewed as an effective means of internal communication. In a survey conducted in late 2016 by the employee communication and engagement agency Gatehouse,[3] 88 per cent of the respondents viewed roadshows with senior leaders as the most effective face-to-face means of internal

---

[3] *State of the Sector, Internal Communication and Employee Engagement*, vol. 9 (2017), a survey of 451 internal communications staff conducted by Gatehouse in November 2016.

communication, with conferences and seminars with managers or senior leaders and team meetings close behind.[4]

When considering digital media, 58 per cent of respondents to the same survey regarded social channels as "very" or "quite" effective, while central emails and electronic newsletters were regarded as effective by 79 and 78 per cent respectively. However, the use of social channels seems due to increase significantly, with three-quarters of respondents[5] intending to increase their use, while a third[6] intended to reduce their use of central emails. The survey concluded that organisations are tending to adopt means of communication which require the employee to be more active in the process of exchanging information: "Self service, it seems, is the order of the day."[7]

However, although self-service methods of employee communication at work echo the growth of social media and other digital approaches in our personal communications, we must never lose sight of the fact that organisations are composed of human beings, and as the Gatehouse survey results show, the most effective communication occurs when one human speaks directly to another. That's not old-fashioned thinking; it's a fact.

We're not naive enough to believe that the CEO of some huge corporation will be able to have a cosy chat with every employee. The larger the organisation, the more difficult it is to achieve a high degree of visibility, but then again, the larger organisations will have more resources and facilities to enable them to create opportunities for some sort of face-to-face contact. A CEO who is content to remain, as far as the employees are concerned, a passport-sized photo on a corporate website or social media page will never

---

[4] 86 per cent and 80 per cent respectively.

[5] 77 per cent.

[6] 34 per cent.

[7] *State of the Sector, Internal Communication and Employee Engagement.*

achieve the degree of communication, contact, and engagement of one who now and then gets out from behind the desk and appears before an audience of some of the living, breathing employees who make his or her organisation tick.

Digital media are there to compensate for the fact that face-to-face contact is more difficult in some organisations, not to entirely replace such contact, or to excuse management from even attempting it.

The focus on well-being

The mental health charity Mind warns that one person in four in the UK will experience a mental health problem each year,[8] and in 2014 the Organisation for Economic Co-operation and Development (OECD) estimated that mental health problems cost Britain £70 billion a year in productivity losses, higher benefit payments, and the increased cost to the NHS. This amounted to 4.5 per cent of GDP.[9] The OECD report also noted that mental health problems were the cause of 40 per cent of the new claims for disability benefit in the UK each year. This is the highest percentage rate of all 34 OECD member nations.

In the light of such damaging consequences, it is extraordinary that many organisations pay so little attention to the mental health of their employees. If a physical illness or injury was the cause of so much disruption and loss of productivity, it would be viewed as a significant threat to the business and be targeted for action, but the importance of mental health is still underestimated by many.

---

[8] S. McManus, H. Meltzer, T. S. Brugha, P. E. Bebbington, and R. Jenkins, *Adult psychiatric morbidity in England, 2007: results of a household survey.* (NHS Digital, 2009), quoted on www.mind.org.uk.

[9] OECD, based on/adapted from *UK needs to tackle high cost of mental-ill health, says OECD,* (1 Oct. 2014), http://www.oecd.org/health/uk-needs-to-tackle-high-cost-of-mental-ill-health.htm, and OECD, *Mental Health and Work: United Kingdom,* OECD Publishing, 2014), http://dx.doi.org/10.1787/9789264204997-en.

"Society would not tolerate an organisation that is unable to look after the physical health and safety of its employees. Equality demands that we apply the same principle to mental health—nothing less is acceptable."[10]

The Heads Together project in the UK, fronted by Prince William and Prince Harry, has done a great deal to not only highlight the importance of addressing mental health problems but also remove some of the stigma which many attach to seeking help when such problems occur.

The President of the Royal College of Psychiatrists, Sir Simon Wessely, said the comments by Prince Harry had achieved more in 25 minutes than he (Sir Simon) had in 25 years, in terms of raising the profile of mental health and the value of counselling. Obviously, any counselling service provided by an enlightened employer will only produce results if people use it, and people support must be the persuaders.

According to the Health and Safety Executive, 11.7 million working days were lost in the UK in 2015–16 due to work-related stress, depression, and anxiety.[11] Any reduction in this huge total can only benefit the organisations concerned, and so, even though the benefit is likely to be impossible to quantify with precision, wellness programmes of all kinds will have a positive effect on the bottom line. Any other factor which produced such a huge loss of productivity would have been addressed long ago. It is only squeamishness on the part of employers, and a reluctance to regard

---

[10] Chartered Institute of Personnel and Development, *Moving the employee well-being agenda forward A collection of thought pieces* (Feb. 2016), with the permission of the publisher, the Chartered Institute of Personnel and Development, https://www.cipd.co.uk/Images/moving-employee-well-being-agenda-forward_2016_tcm18-15556.pdf.

[11] Health and Safety Executive, *Work related stress, anxiety and depression statistics in Great Britain*, (2016), http://www.hse.gov.uk/statistics/causdis/stress/.

conditions such as stress and depression as "real illnesses", which has prevented action being taken more widely.

"There is a wealth of evidence in the academic and non-academic literature that suggests a positive link between the introduction of wellness programmes in the workplace and improved business key performance indicators. The available literature suggests that programme costs can quickly be translated into financial benefits, either through cost savings or additional revenue generation, as a consequence of the improvement in a wide range of intermediate business measures."[12]

As the CIPD states: "If employers place employee well-being at the centre of their business model and view it as the vital source of value-creation, the dividends for organisational health can be significant."[13]

A study undertaken in the UK by PricewaterhouseCoopers LLP in 2008[14] found that 45 out of 55 organisations consulted reported a reduction in sickness absence because of wellness interventions, with an average reduction of 30 to 40 per cent. Some organisations also reported reductions in staff turnover and accidents at work, while others experienced an increase in staff satisfaction and productivity.

Wellness programmes are no longer solely the province of wacky Californian IT firms; they make good business sense for all types of organisations. A wise business which depends on the use of vehicles, for example, will have them serviced to keep them in good condition, because breakdowns can be expensive and disrupt operations. An

[12] PricewaterhouseCoopers, *Building the case for wellness* (2008).

[13] Chartered Institute of Personnel and Development, *Moving the employee well-being agenda forward*, with the permission of the publisher, the Chartered Institute of Personnel and Development (www.cipd.co.uk)

[14] PricewaterhouseCoopers, *Building the case for wellness* (2008).

equally wise business will do everything possible to ensure that its *people* remain in the best possible physical and mental health. As well as being the *right* thing to do, it is also the sensible, business-like thing to do, because it benefits the bottom line.

Helping employees to stop smoking, for example, would once have been seen as outside the responsibility of any employer, but there are sound business reasons for including smoking cessation in any wellness programme. Research published in the UK in 2006[15] showed that a smoker costs an employer an average of 64 minutes per day in lost productivity, as a result of the time taken on smoke breaks. Encouraging employees to give up smoking could thus gain an hour's work a day per smoker, a significant boost to productivity, as well as being a long-term investment in improving their health. As the researchers concluded: "In-house, occupational health-led smoking cessation initiatives have the potential to make a positive impact in terms of company productivity as well as employee health."[16]

According to estimates from the Department of Work and Pensions, by 2024 nearly half of the UK population will be aged 50 or over, and increases in the pension age mean that organisations of all kinds will soon find themselves with older employees than they have ever had before. As a result, the provision of health-related services of all kinds will become even more important, and promoting good mental and physical health among employees, as well as a healthy work–life balance, will be crucial to the success of any organisation.

---

[15] Ryan and Crampin, "Time *cost associated with smoking at work highlighted by baseline survey of employees participating in a workplace smoking cessation programme*", *Occupational Medicine* (Oct. 2006).
[16] Ryan and Crampin, "Time *cost associated with smoking at work highlighted by baseline survey of employees participating in a workplace smoking cessation programme*", *Occupational Medicine* (Oct. 2006).

What needs to be encouraged goes beyond mindfulness or single initiatives. The research by Dr. Andre Vermeulen in South Africa on neuro-agility highlights the complexity of brain fitness and the drivers and factors that can be trained and developed to enhance it. The inclusion of physical fitness opportunities, relaxing and regenerative programmes all impact workplace energy and productivity.

The people support/HR profession has the responsibility to ensure that organisations adopt practices which promote wellness in the broadest sense, and to ensure the highest possible take-up of any schemes introduced. People support professionals hold the vital middle ground, in a position both to influence management in adopting wellness programmes and to encourage employees to use them.

"The HR profession holds the key to unlocking the potential for a much wider and more sustainable integration of health and well-being practices at work. HR professionals are in a unique position to steer the health and well-being agenda in organisations and drive a systemic approach, including ensuring that senior managers regard it as a priority, and that employee well-being practices are integrated in the organisation's day-to-day operations."[17]

So what?

The field of employee relations embraces a growing range of activities, which is reflected in the emergence of an internal communications specialisation. It is no longer so much a matter of negotiations with trade unions as the maintenance of relationships with individual employees and, in some organisations at least, a concern with individual health and well-being.

---

[17] Chartered Institute of Personnel and Development, *Moving the employee well-being agenda forward* (2016), with the permission of the publisher, the Chartered Institute of Personnel and Development,(www.cipd.co.uk).

The rapid growth of social media has been mirrored within organisations by significant improvements in employee voice, the ability of employees to have a say in the way their organisations are run. Enterprise social networks have developed as a means of encouraging employees to express their opinions, enabling a crowdsourcing approach to business communication and problem solving. This is an effective and fast-moving method of maintaining communication between widely-dispersed groups of employees, but it is not everyone's cup of tea, so it is essential to ensure that other methods are available, or that training is provided, so as not to leave some staff behind in the move towards digital methods of communication. The use of digital media must not be used as an excuse to absolve managers, including the most senior, from the duty to get out among the people who work for them. 'Management by walking about' and 'catching them doing good' still work!

Wellness programmes are becoming more common, acknowledging the fact that it is not just desirable but also sound business practice to make efforts to safeguard employees' physical and mental health. The losses in productivity caused by both physical and mental illness are enormous. Addressing these problems will have a tangible impact on the bottom line. The inclusion of mental health in this equation is relatively recent but long overdue. Comments by Prince Harry in particular will help enormously in breaking down the stigma previously attached to seeking help. Addressing the mental health of employees is just as important as preventing industrial accidents or work-related illnesses.

Increases in the pension age will lead to organisations having older employees on their books than ever before, and so matters of health are destined to become increasingly important.

CONCLUSIONS

go beyond—achieve "impact
people support" to create
your workplace = your world

People support in the immediate future will be as important within the people support teams as within the organisations they serve. Transformation and change add to pressures and the urgency to adapt and meet the unique needs of your organisation through rapid insight and enhanced impact, and the effort to deliver real value to your organisation's flow will stretch the resilience of many. In meeting these challenges, the opportunities to embrace technology, and the impacts of cultural development and globalisation, are as never before. We must go beyond what we know now to reach what we need to know to meet the challenges facing organisations of any size and the people working within them.

Start with the business. *Gain deep insight.* Ultimately the need is for high energy, focused energy, understanding and encouraging workplaces that maximise productivity and performance. Starting with appreciating all the contributory factors and drivers behind these, such as levels of engagement, detachment, resilience, collaboration, motivation and beyond, will help determine necessary strategies for support, development and improving or transforming change and performance. Insights can be gained from unique surveys and when doing so, ensure any surveys provide deep and meaningful data that cannot be misinterpreted. For example, a manager deciding that person A highlighted they were wanting more responsibility but was wrong could mean that person A may take it badly and is set up to fail, and then also upsets person B who really wanted it, and also quickly disconnects what was previously an engaged team.

The quality of analysis and reporting is key to gaining greater understanding through providing insight. A 360-degree assessment is not necessarily a good 360-degree assessment! HR/people support has spent far too long speaking its own language without ensuring that its message was being understood. *Speak the language of your business and of the people in it.*

Add to insight with your own operational excellence; *being aligned, integrated, well managed, efficient, credible, and effective; reporting impact; being conscious of the possible; and enabling flow, trust, and performance.*

Go beyond common practice, the stuff you have always done, the vendor research, the misplaced assumptions, and the bandwagon. Generate energy, reduce stress, enhance performance, and support the people who will make the difference and achieve the results you need. Go beyond engagement to include detachment, readiness-to-change, and motivation factors. Explore the consequences and related impact on customers, the influence of management, and the value created by team and departments. Enable performance for achievement; don't simply manage to judge. Do what your organisation, and the people within, needs, not what others are doing. This is true for all sectors, all industries, and all people; however, it should be uniquely yours: YOUR WORKPLACE = YOUR WORLD.

Impact people support: Our concluding ten steps for meeting future challenges

Go Beyond has sought to explore the many challenges facing all within people specialist roles. We have assumed that the "defensive" elements of personnel report (record-keeping, sickness and absence management, and company statistics relating to equality and inclusion, payroll, and health and safety) will continue to be a necessary function and service that is delivered as efficiently as possible and creates the minimum disruption for all involved. The challenges of perception, sense of value, impact, generating performance to new levels, creating required culture and consistency in application of values, talent, market shortages, digitalisation, technology, artificial intelligence, commerciality (including nonprofits), and more will all require high standards of functional integration, informed decision-making, collaboration, and coordination. The People in Flow Department 360 Assessment provides a framework for insight into the current and potential future perception. From what we have discussed, considered, researched, and shared within this book, we note now some of the key factors and checks required in moving towards providing impact people support:

1. **Go beyond HR and say what you *are*—whether you use "people support and development" or a similar term.**
    - Ensure there are no unintended consequences.
        o Human Resources may have reputational problems. Where does it really stand in your organisation?
        o What is it called?

- Language matters! Reflect what you are for—just as marketing, sales, and finance do.
- Frameworks need to ensure and enable *people* contribution.
- *You* are part of *the* business/organisation.

2. **Go beyond your department and start with the rest of the business.**
   - Alignment is key.
   - Go beyond the HR agenda.
   - Your organisation is uniquely yours, and you are part of it.
   - Go beyond being just as expected in your own leadership: align, integrate, manage, impact.

3. **Go beyond analytics and explore the story.**
   - Go beyond the metrics of Personnel
   - What is happening?
   - The question comes first.
   - So what?
   - Find the why, what, who, when, where, and how—in that order!
   - Provide insight – beyond knowledge to applied wisdom.
   - Smash the silos.
   - Who are the data champions?
   - Enable predictive analytics (only 4 per cent of UK organisations do so!).
   - What matters? What behaviours will drive optimal results (going beyond the gross intent score!)?

4. **Go beyond engagement and value your people.**
   - Motivation
     - o AMP
     - o Positive wiring
     - o To whose benefit?
     - o Contribution awareness
     - o Recognition
   - Two-way checks

- What are your management balance sheets?
- Detachment is beyond non-engagement.
- Communication is never too much. Why the secret?
- Resilience and change readiness is a consequence.
- Wellness
  - o This is essential, not merely desirable.
  - o Go beyond simply providing gimmicks and apps.
  - o Explore mindsets.
  - o Go beyond the physical to include brain fitness and mental well-being.
  - o Reduce stress.

5. **Go beyond process and enable flow.**
   - Be clear on where everyone adds value.
   - Explore where they could add further value.
   - Put people back into the lean processes.
   - Ensure that the right people are in the right seats facing the right way and doing the right things.

6. **Go beyond performance management to enablement.**
   - What do you need?
   - Explore your intended impact grids.
   - Consider instant objectives.
   - Ensure clarity of responsibility.
   - Enable performance; achieve results.
   - Energise your workplace.

7. **Go beyond training and learning to achieve impact and enhance neuro-agility**
   - Start with undertanding your brain drivers and neuro-design
   - Encourage personal responsibility and utilise Personal Learning and Performance Playbooks.
   - In doing so, ensure the personal blend and opportunity is supported by provision of access media options — go beyond single strategies.

- Clarify support and guidance responsibility.
- Learning needs risk—relevance, interest, skills(mindset and application), knowledge.
- Motivate employees to learn and perform.
- Allow the learning-to-performance flow—go beyond transfer.
- Achieve functional mastery—ensure your own development and credibility.
- Go beyond talent management and enable optimal growth for all.
  - What have you got?
  - What happened after Day 1?
  - Do you have what you need now?
  - Is everyone in the right seat, doing the right things in the right way?
  - What will you need?
  - How are you developing talent in a collaborative and coordinated way?
  - Go beyond the subjective.

8. **Go beyond recruitment and build your corporate team.**
   - Make it matter.
   - Go beyond ticking boxes.
   - Be clear on your culture, your values, and who will fit.
   - Get who fits and who will also add value.
   - Ensure that their welcome enables them to add their value.
   - Be brave.

9. **Go beyond jargon, and communicate with conviction.**
   - Talk the right talk.
   - Be clear on difference.
   - Embrace difference.
   - Be thorough.
   - Repeat and enhance.

10. **Finally, just simply go beyond—and do what you need to do.**

Do this by going beyond:
- Fads
- Tradition and "common" practice. Be innovative and apply action to your unique organisation with and for your people.
- Compliance. Create impact and flow from insight.
- "Solutioneering" (the practice of deciding the answer and seeking the question later).
- Manager-led assumptions. Be who you are *for* who you are by applying expertise to rapid, appropriate, and deep insight.
- Valued to be valuable. Add value as individuals, teams, and departments, and be experts.
- Standard reporting. Measure what matters. Analyse, and report the story.
- Ticking boxes. Align and integrate, manage and lead with credibility by being efficient and commercial, effective and creating impact, and be conscious of the possible.

REFERENCES AND SOURCES OF INSPIRATION

Foreword

Grint, K., "Wicked *problems and clumsy solutions: the role of* leadership", *Clinical Leader*, 1/2 (2008), 11–25.

Heifetz, R., A. Grashow, and M. Linsky, "Leadership in a Permanent Crisis", *Harvard Business Review*, 87 (July–August 2009), 62–69.

Johansen, B., *Get there early: Sensing the future to compete in the present.* 2007, (San Francisco: Berrett-Koehler, 2007).

Vaill, P. B., *Learning as a way of being: strategies for survival in a world of permanent whitewater.* 1996, (San Francisco: Jossey-Bass, 1996).

Chapter 1

Brinkerhoff, Robert, impact maps in *Success Case Method* (2005). Ceplenski, Chris, "Employee Rewards: The Importance of Perceived Fairness", *HR Daily Advisor* (June 2013).

Charan, Ram, "It's Time to Split HR", *Harvard Business Review* (2014).

Chartered Institute of Personnel and Development, *The Changing Contours of Fairness* (4 Nov. 2013).

Chartered Institute of Personnel and Development, *Learning and Development*, annual survey report (2015), https://www.cipd.co.uk/Images/learning-development_2015_tcm18-11298.pdf, accessed May 2017.

Corporate Research Forum, *Developing Commercial Acumen* (2013).

Deloitte Consulting, *Global Human Capital Trends 2015: Leading in the New World of Work* (Deloitte University Press, 2015).

Deloitte Consulting, *Global Human Capital Trends 2016: The* new organization: Different by *design* (Deloitte University Press, 2016).

Efron, Louis, "How AI Is About to Disrupt Corporate Recruiting", *Forbes* (12 July 2016), https://www.forbes.com/sites/louisefron/2016/07/12/how-a-i-is-about-to-disrupt-corporate-recruiting/#159b772b3ba2.

Evans, Alex, *The Myth Gap* (Eden Project Books, 2017).

Jacobs, Susanne, "Why fairness" affects staff performance", *People Management* (Aug. 2013).

KPMG and the Economist Intelligence Unit, *Rethinking Human Resources in a Changing World* (2013).

Lewis, Grace, "HR 'lacks skills to become more strategic' despite major changes", *People Management* (13 Feb. 2013).

PricewaterhouseCoopers, Annual Global CEO Survey (2015).

PricewaterhouseCoopers, Annual Global CEO Survey (2012).

PricewaterhouseCoopers, *Delivering more for less. What sets top performers part?* (2014).

Senge, Peter, *The Fifth Discipline: The* art and practice of the learning organization (2nd edn, Random House Business, 2006).

Sparrow et al, "Do We Need HR?", *HR Magazine* (2015).

Towards Maturity, *Embracing Change, 2015–16 Annual Benchmark Report* (Nov. 2015), www.towardsmaturity.org/2015benchmark.

Ulrich, Dave, *Human Resource Champions* (Harvard Business School Press, 1997).

Chapter 2

Adie, Kate, *Fighting on the Home Front: The Legacy of Women in World War One* (Hodder Paperbacks, 2013).

Arets, Jos and Charles Jennings, *70:20:10 Towards 100% performance* (2016).

Armstrong, M., *A Handbook of Personnel Management Practice* (Kogan Page, 1995).

Bersin by Deloitte, *UK Corporate Learning Factbook 2016: Benchmarks, Trends, and Analysis of the UK Training* Market (2016).

Burns, Detert, and Chiaburu, "Quitting before leaving: the mediating effects of psychological attachment and detachment on voice", *Journal of Applied Psychology* (July 2008).

Cannon, James A., and Rita McGee, *Talent Management and Succession Planning* (2nd edn, London, CIPD, 2010).

Chartered Institute of Personnel and Development, *Employee Outlook* (Autumn 2016), https://www.cipd.co.uk/Images/employee-outlook_2016-autumn_tcm18-16797.pdf.

CIPD with Towards Maturity, *L&D: Evolving Roles, enhancing skills*, Research report (Apr. 2015).

Chartered Institute of Personnel and Development, *Resourcing and Talent Planning* (2015), https://www.cipd.co.uk/Images/resourcing-talent-planning_2015_tcm18-11303.pdf.

Churchard, Claire, "Appraisals Deemed *unfair by one-third of employees, finds CIPD"*, *People Management* (May 2014).

Collins, Jim, *Good to Great* (1st edn, Curtis Brown, 2001).

Crim, Dan, and Gerard Seijts, "What Engages Employees the Most or the Ten Cs of Employee Engagement", *Ivey Business Journal* (Mar.–Apr. 2006).

Department for Business, Energy, and Industrial Strategy, *Engaging for Success: enhancing performance through employee engagement*, Department for Business, Energy and Industrial Strategy, 2009

Dzubian, Hartman, and Moskal, *Blended Learning* (University of Central Florida, 2004).

Economist Intelligence Unit on behalf of the Chartered Institute of Management Accountants (CIMA) and the American Institute of Certified Public Accountants (AICPA), *Talent Pipeline Draining Growth* (2012).

Ferguson, Owen, Stef Scott, and Gemma Towersey, *Learning Technologies: What Managers Really Think*, (Good Practice, Nov. 2017).

Frith, Beckett, "What Brexit Means for HR", *HR Magazine* (24 June 2016), http://www.hrmagazine.co.uk/article-details/what-brexit-means-for-hr.

Gratton, Lynda, *The Shift* (William Collins, 2014).

Groysberg, Nohria, and Fernandez-Araoz, "The Definitive Guide to Recruiting in Good Times and Bad", *Harvard Business Review* (May 2009).

Holmes, Andy, *Social Media and the Engaged Employee* (HR in Flow, 2017).

Human Capital Media, "2016 Survey of Measurement and Metrics", *Chief Learning Officer* (2016).

Hopping, Clare, "Making Selection Easier with Automated Recruitment", *Launch Pad Recruits*, http://www.launchpadrecruits.com/insight-articles/automated-recruitment.

Institute of Employment Studies, *The Drivers of Employee Engagement*, Report No. 408 (2004).

Johnson, Mike, *The New Rules of Engagement* (Chartered Institute of Personnel and Development, 2004).

Kontakos, Anne-Marie, "Seeing Clearly: Employee Engagement and Line of Sight", in *Employee Engagement: What Do We Really Know? What Do We Need to Know to Take Action?* (Cornell University's Center for Advanced Human Resource Studies, 2007).

KPMG and the Economist Intelligence Unit, *Rethinking Human Resources in a Changing World* (2012).

Learning and Performance Institute, *The LPI Capability Map: Six-Month Report* (June 2013).

McIlvaine, Andrew, "Brexit: The Human Resource Implications", *HRE Daily* (30 June 2016) http://blog.hreonline.com/2016/06/30/brexit-the-hr-implications/.

O'Leonard, Karen, *The UK Learning Factbook 2013: Benchmarks, Trends, and Analysis of the UK Training Market* (Bersin by Deloitte, 2013).

Philpott, William, *Attrition: Fighting the First World War* (Abacus, 2014).

Potter, Amanda, and Sarah Linton, *The Future of Talent Management* (Zircon Management Consulting, May 2012).

Robertson-Smith, Gemma, and Carl Markwick, *Employee Engagement: A Review of Current Thinking*, Institute of Employment Studies Report 469 (2009).

Ryan, Liz, "How Technology Killed Recruiting", *Forbes* (9 Jan. 2014). https://www.forbes.com/sites/lizryan/2014/01/29/how-technology-killed-recruiting/#2a1c0d6b590f.

State of the Sector, Internal Communication and Employee Engagement, vol. 9, 2017 (Gatehouse, Nov. 2016).

Sulivan, John, "The Top 12 Reasons Why Slow Hiring Severely Damages Recruiting and Business Results", *ERE Recruiting Intelligence* (21 Apr. 2014), https://www.eremedia.com/ere/the-top-12-reasons-why-slow-hiring-severely-damages-recruiting-and-business-results/.

UK Commission for Employment and Skills, Employer Skills Survey 2015 (May 2016).

Towers Watson, *How to Build a Compelling Employee Value Proposition* (Jan. 2014).

Chapter 3

Accenture, *Analytics in Action: Breakthroughs and Barriers on the Journey to ROI* (2013).

Chartered Institute of Personnel and Development, *HR Analytics* (May 2017), www.cipd.co.uk/knowledge/strategy/analytics/factsheet.

Chartered Institute of Personnel and Development, *HR Outlook: Winter 2016–17: Views of Our Profession*, https://www.cipd.co.uk/Images/hr-outlook_2017_tcm18-17697.pdf.

Chartered Institute of Personnel and Development, *Talent Analytics and Big Data – the challenge for HR*, (November 2013).

Holley, Nick, *Big Data and HR* Henley Centre for HR Excellence, Henley Business School, University of Reading (2013)

Chapter 4

Bowles, Hannah Riley, "Why Women Don't Negotiate Their Job Offers", *Harvard Business Review* (19 June 2014).

Chartered Institute of Personnel and Development, *Bonuses and incentives: Learn how to design and operate and effective bonus or incentive scheme* (1 Mar. 2016), https://www.cipd.co.uk/knowledge/fundamentals/people/pay/bonuses-factsheet.

"CIPD welcomes first steps in repairing UK's broken executive pay system" (Nov. 2016), https://www.cipd.co.uk/about/media/press/repairing-executive-pay-system.

Clapp, Kathryn, and Kate Whelan, "'Hot topic: Gender pay gap reporting, part two", *HR Magazine* (Apr. 2017).

Correll, Shelley J., Stephen Benard, and In Paik, "Getting a Job: Is There a Motherhood Penalty?" *American Journal of Sociology*, 112/5 (2007), 1297–1339, retrieved from Harvard Kennedy School Women and Public Policy Program's Gender Action portal, http://gap.hks.harvard.edu/getting-job-there-motherhood-penalty.

Department for Business, Energy, and Industrial Strategy, *Corporate Governance Reform: Green Paper* (Nov. 2016).

Easton, Carole, and Maggie Stilwell, "Hot topic: Gender pay gap reporting', *HR Magazine* (Apr. 2017).

Ernst and Young, Employment Tax Alert, *Weight Watchers— Employment Status* (2011).

Farber, Madeline, "3 Reasons Why the Gender Pay Gap Still Exists", *Fortune* (Apr. 2017).

Linklaters, *European Parliament votes on CRD 4, including bonus cap* (Apr. 2013).

O'Donnell, Kathleen, "Bonuses—the Good and the Bad", *Off the Cusp* (6 Mar. 2014).

Rodionova, Zlata, "Theresa May Could force companies to reveal pay gap between executives and average workers", *The Independent* (29 Nov. 2016).

Chapter 5

Chartered Institute of Personnel and Development, Moving the employee well-being agenda forward. A collection of thought pieces (Feb. 2016), https://www.cipd.co.uk/Images/moving-employee-well-being-agenda-forward_2016_tcm18-15556.pdf.

Chartered Institute of Personnel and Development, *Social media and employee voice: the current landscape,* CIPD, 2013 < social-media-and-employee-voice_2013-current-landscape-sop_tcm18-10327.pdf.

Financial Services Authority, "A regulatory response to the global banking crisis", Discussion Paper 9/2 (Mar. 2009).

Health and Safety Executive, *Work- related stress, anxiety and depression statistics in Great Britain* (2016), http://www.hse.gov.uk/statistics/causdis/stress/.

McManus, S., H. Meltzer, T. S. Brugha, P. E. Bebbington, and R. Jenkins, "Adult psychiatric morbidity in England, 2007: results of a household survey" (2009), *NHS Digital*, quoted on www.mind.org.uk.

OECD, "High Cost of Mental Ill-Health",: Based on/Adapted from OECD (2014), "UK Needs to tackle high cost of mental-ill health, says OECD" (1 Oct. 2014), http://www.oecd.org/health/uk-needs-to-tackle-high-cost-of-mental-ill-health.htm.

OECD *Mental Health and Work: United Kingdom* (Paris, OECD Publishing, 2014), http://dx.doi.org/10.1787/9789264204997-en.

PricewaterhouseCoopers, *Building the case for wellness* (2008).

Ryan and Crampin, "Time cost associated with smoking at work highlighted by baseline survey of employees participating in a workplace smoking cessation programme, *Occupational Medicine* (Oct. 2006).

"What is leadership: in the HR hot seat *HR Magazine*. Weblog post available at http://content.yudu.com/Library/A1uvje/HRMagazineDecember20/resources/17.htm.

*   *   *

ABOUT THE AUTHORS

Neville Pritchard, CEO of People in Flow Ltd

Having worked in senior and executive people support roles at Legal & General, Abbey National, and Barclays, Neville co-founded INL Consultancy Ltd in 2005. He established HR in Flow in 2013.

Neville is a Chartered Fellow of the Chartered Institute of Personnel and Development, a Fellow of the Learning and Performance Institute, a Fellow of the Chartered Institute of Bankers, and Member of the European Mentoring and Coaching Council.

He was chairman of the Association for Talent Development International Conference Programme Committee in 2015, and a reviewer for the ATD BEST Awards, 2007–2016. He was a judge for the Training Journal Awards for 2017, and was previously chairman of the FSSC Major Employer Advisory Forum and a board member of the Institute of Financial Services Schools faculty, 2002 and 2005.

Neville has been married to his wife, Eszter, for 36 years, with two sons, Dominic and Robin. Beyond work, he is a keen sportsman and has played and coached rugby and cricket, has managed the Bucks Academy Cricket side, and now represents Buckinghamshire in seniors cricket. He is also a trustee for the Bucks Youth Cricket Trust. Neville began his career in teaching before moving to financial services.

Richard Scott, Chief Researcher, People in Flow Ltd

Richard served as an air traffic controller in the RAF. He subsequently worked in L&D roles in the Civil Service, and then as a police intelligence analyst, before joining HR in Flow in his role as chief researcher.

In his wider role, he ensures that the consulting teams of HR in Flow and People in Flow are consistently up to date, are globally conscious, and are constantly exploring new ways of thinking and acting, thereby ensuring they work to maximise the value of people-related functions within organisations.

Richard has also for many years been a governor of the grammar school in Devon which both he and Neville attended. Outside work and the school, Richard is an avid student of military history, especially the First World War and the Royal Air Force. He is also a keen photographer, specialising in the landscapes and seascapes of his native Devon.

People in Flow